THE ART OF
MIXOLOGY

THE ART OF
MIXOLOGY

CLASSIC COCKTAILS AND CURIOUS CONCOCTIONS

This edition published by
Cottage Door Press, LLC, in 2018.
First published 2015 by Parragon Books, Ltd.

Copyright © 2018 Cottage Door Press, LLC
5005 Newport Drive, Rolling Meadows, Illinois 60008

New recipes by Kim Davies
New photography by Mike Cooper

ISBN: 978-1-68052-410-9

Printed in China

Love Food™ is an imprint of Cottage Door Press, LLC.
Parragon Books® and the Parragon® logo are registered
trademarks of Cottage Door Press, LLC.

Notes for the Reader

This book uses standard kitchen measuring spoons and
cups. All spoon and cup measurements are level unless
otherwise indicated. Unless otherwise stated, milk
is assumed to be whole, eggs are large, individual
vegetables are medium, and pepper is freshly ground
black pepper. Unless otherwise stated, all root
vegetables should be peeled prior to using. People
with nut allergies should be aware that some of the
prepared ingredients used in the recipes in this book
may contain nuts.

Garnishes, decorations, and serving suggestions are
all optional and not necessarily included in the recipe
ingredients or method. The times given are only an
approximate guide. Preparation times differ according
to the techniques used by different people and the
cooking times may also vary from those given. Optional
ingredients, variations, or serving suggestions have
not been included in the time calculations.

Please consume alcohol responsibly.

CONTENTS

PAGE 6

INTRODUCTION

∞

PAGE 16

GIN & VODKA

∞

PAGE 54

RUM, WHISKIES
& BRANDY

∞

PAGE 88

BUBBLES
(BOTH NAUGHTY & NICE)

∞

PAGE 122

SOMETHING DIFFERENT

∞

PAGE 156

MOCKTAILS

This beautiful book, with its delicious recipes and appealing photography, will quickly become an indispensable tool for the budding mixologist. In this comprehensive collection, you'll find punches for parties, short drinks for unwinding in the evening, and impressive crowd pleasers for entertaining. All of the recipes are simply written to make them easy to follow, and even novice cocktail makers are guaranteed a winning result every time.

INTRODUCTION

Cocktails have played a colorful part in modern history and have established their place in popular culture. The history of the first cocktail remains a mystery, which has led to a number of entertaining folk tales. One of the more popular stories tells how, during the Revolutionary War, American and French soldiers frequented Betsy's Tavern to enjoy a famous alcoholic concoction of her own creation, known as "Betsy's Bracer." One night, amid a whirl of wild drinking and parties, one of the American soldiers stole a couple of cockerels from a neighbor's yard. He toasted his theft with his drinking companions, saying, "Here's to the divine liquor which is as delicious to the palate as the cock's tail is beautiful to the eye." A French officer is said to have responded to the toast with a rousing cry of "Vive le cocktail!"—and with that, the term cocktail was born.

Since their conception, cocktail trends have come and gone—from the days of the practical cocktail (mixers were used to disguise the sometimes coarse flavors of homemade liquors during the Prohibition era), to the fancy, frivolous cocktails favored during the 1980s, and the pared-back, stylish cocktails made famous by stage and screen characters at the start of this century.

The art of the skilled mixologist is based on easy-to-follow principles that can set almost anyone on the right track to producing an impressive range of cocktails and mixed drinks. This book will give you all the skills you need, and you can apply these to the whole range of cocktail recipes here. Simply read up on the terminology and techniques that follow and get started on the recipes—before long, you'll soon be mixing and shaking with the best of them.

ESSENTIAL EQUIPMENT

COCKTAIL SHAKER

Cocktail shakers come in several sizes; choose one that can hold at least 16 ounces. Look for one that has a double lid, which incorporates a perforated strainer. If yours does not have an integral strainer, you will need a separate one.

MIXING GLASS

This is used for making stirred cocktails. You can use any large container or pitcher, or you can buy professional mixing glasses.

STRAINER

A bar or Hawthorn strainer is the perfect tool to prevent ice and other ingredients from being poured from the shaker or mixing glass into the serving glass. You could use a small nylon strainer instead.

BAR SPOON

This long-handle spoon is used for stirring cocktails in a mixing glass.

JIGGER

This hourglass-shape cocktail measuring device often has a standard jigger "measure" of 1½ ounces on one end and 1 ounce, or a "pony," on the other end; 1 (fluid) ounce is the same as 2 tablespoons. As long as you keep the proportions of the various ingredients the same, you can use a jigger of another size—it is the porportions, not the specific quantities, that are crucial.

MUDDLER

This miniature masher is used for crushing ingredients, such as herbs, in the bottom of a glass. You can also use a mortar and pestle.

OTHER EQUIPMENT

Equipment that is useful includes: a corkscrew, a citrus reamer and zester, cutting boards, knives, pitchers, ice buckets and tongs, and a blender for creamy cocktails and slushes. Optional extras include cocktail toothpicks, swizzle sticks, and straws.

MARTINI GLASS

The most immediately recognizable cocktail glass, the Martini glass has a conical shape that helps stop the ingredients from separating, while the stem keeps the drink cool.

MARGARITA GLASS

This glass is based on the earlier champagne coupe that was originally used for serving bubbly. The wide bowl is perfect for adding salt to the rim, making it the ideal glass, of course, for serving Margaritas.

HURRICANE GLASS

The shape of this large, short-stemmed glass is said to resemble the hurricane lamp, from which it gets its name. It was originally used for the famous Hurricane cocktail at Pat O'Brien's bar in New Orleans, but today it's more usually associated with exotic frozen and blended cocktails.

CHAMPAGNE FLUTE

The tapered shape of this tall, thin glass is designed to reduce the surface area of the liquid, keeping the champagne bubbly for longer.

HIGHBALL GLASS

Highball glasses are tall and suitable for simple drinks that have a high proportion of mixer to liquor. They are versatile enough to be substituted for the similar, but slightly larger, Collins glass.

OLD-FASHIONED GLASS

The terms "old-fashioned," "rocks," and "lowball" are often used to refer to short, squat glasses with a heavy bottom. They are perfect for holding ice and are used to serve any liquor "on the rocks." They are also useful for short mixed drinks.

SHOT GLASS

A home-bar essential, the shot glass holds just enough liquid to be downed in a single mouthful. Shot glasses have thick bottoms so that they can withstand being slammed on the bar.

IRISH COFFEE GLASS

The two key features of an Irish coffee glass are heatproof glass and a handle, both of which make it suitable for hot cocktails, such as toddies.

MIXING METHODS

Creating a cocktail is not brain surgery, but it does require the deft touch of a skilled mixologist. The better your mixing techniques, the better the quality of the cocktail. Mixing a cocktail is not just a matter of throwing all the ingredients together in a glass, giving them a stir, and hoping for the best. There are many different mixing methods, all of which have benefits. The following are the most commonly used methods and the ones that you will find in this book.

SHAKING

This is when you add all the ingredients, with a scoop of ice, to the shaker and then shake vigorously for approximately 5 seconds. The benefit of shaking is that the drink is rapidly mixed, chilled, and aerated; after the drink has been shaken, the outside of the shaker will be lightly frosted. Shaking a cocktail also dilutes the drink significantly. This dilution is a necessary part of the cocktail-making process and gives shaken recipes the correct balance of taste, strength, and temperature.

In addition, shaking can be used to prepare cocktails that include an ingredient, such as egg white, that will not combine effectively with the other ingredients if you use a less vigorous form of mixing.

STIRRING

Once again, you add all the ingredients to a scoop of ice, but this time you combine them in a mixing glass or small pitcher and then stir the ingredients together using a long-handled bar spoon or stirrer.

As with shaking, this lets you blend and chill the ingredients but without too much erosion of the ice, so you can control the level of dilution and keep it to a minimum.

This simple but vital technique is essential for drinks that don't need a lot of dilution, such as a classic Dry Martini.

BUILDING

To "build" a drink, you simply make it in the glass, for example, in the same way that you make a gin and tonic. It is important to follow the instructions for built cocktails to the letter, because the order of ingredients can change from drink to drink and this can affect the finished flavor.

MUDDLING

Muddling is the term used to describe the extraction of the juice or oils from the pulp or skin of a fruit, herb, or spice. A muddler is simply a pestle used to crush the ingredient. You can buy a specific cocktail muddler, or just use the end of a wooden spoon.

BLENDING

As the name suggests, this is when the ingredients are combined in a blender. Most blended drinks will have a smooth consistency. The ingredients are usually blended with a scoop of crushed ice and often include items that can't be shaken or stirred, such as fresh fruit.

LAYERING

When creating layers in a cocktail, you should follow the instructions carefully, putting the heavier liquors or liqueurs into the glass first. If you add them in the wrong order, you may find that one layer "bleeds" into the next, ruining the look of your cocktail. The first, bottom layer should be poured into the center of the glass, without getting any down the sides, if possible. To create the second layer, turn a teaspoon upside down, with the tip touching the inside of the glass, then pour the liquid slowly over the back of the spoon (moving it up the glass as the level rises). Repeat with any remaining liquid ingredients, using a clean teaspoon to pour each new layer.

STYLE & FLAIR

Ice is incredibly important in the world of cocktail mixing. Get it right and you have the basis of an amazing cocktail; get it wrong, it can make a great drink just average. The ice does two things: during the mixing process it helps to chill and actively mixes the ingredients, and once the drink is served, it keeps the cocktail cold and prevents too much additional dilution. This book uses three types of ice in the cocktail recipes, each with distinctive properties that complement the styles and flavors of the drinks.

ICE CUBES

These are generally used to finish a drink. The more ice you have in your glass, the colder and less diluted your finished cocktail will be. Ice cubes can be made in the freezer in an ice tray; ¾-inch cubes are the best size for finishing most drinks. The cubes can be broken down and used to make cracked and crushed ice, as necessary.

CRUSHED ICE

This is perfect for blended drinks, because it speeds up the mixing process and freezes the whole concoction rapidly. Crushed or cracked ice is better for some drinks, because you can pack the glass with the maximum amount of ice (cubes leave greater gaps). To make crushed ice, wrap ice cubes in a dry dish towel and bang with a rolling pin to break into small pieces.

CRACKED ICE

This is smaller than full ice cubes and is generally used in a shaker to chill the liquid ingredients before you strain them. To make cracked ice from whole cubes, simply wrap the cubes in a dry dish towel and give them a gentle bang with a rolling pin—4-6 ice cubes is enough for making a cocktail to serve one. The ice should be broken into pieces no smaller than half a cube.

THE GARNISH

Many people consider the garnish the thing that defines a cocktail. In some cases, your choice of garnish can reflect the drink itself— think of the Piña Colada with its obligatory pineapple slice. Sometimes the garnish is a vital ingredient, but it's usually just added to make the drink look more attractive.

THE FINAL FLOURISH

There are basic guidelines for adding the final
touches to a drink, but ultimately the way in
which you garnish a cocktail will often be the
result of your imagination and artistic flair.

One of the simplest rules to follow is to
match the garnish to the main flavors
of the cocktail. Think of your cocktail as a
blank canvas. In this book, we recommend some
simple garnishes to go with the recipes,
but if you want to have some fun, throw
the rule book in the trash can and try
creating your own.

Remember: Enjoy your drinks, but don't
make yourself sick and be aware of current
government guidelines on alcohol consumption.
Experiment to your heart's content with this
book and get the maximum pleasure out of your
cocktails by following the recipes, perfecting
and using the tried and tested mixing methods,
and using the right glass for whatever cocktail
you are making. Then just garnish and enjoy.

GIN & VODKA

SERVES 1

INGREDIENTS

2½ OUNCES GIN

1 TEASPOON DRY VERMOUTH,
OR TO TASTE

COCKTAIL OLIVE, TO GARNISH

MARTINI

1. Put cracked ice into a cocktail shaker.

2. Pour the gin and vermouth over the ice.

3. Shake until well frosted. Strain into a chilled cocktail glass.

4. Garnish with the olive. Serve immediately.

SERVES 1

INGREDIENTS

1¼ OUNCES GIN

¾ OUNCE CHERRY BRANDY

¾ OUNCE LEMON JUICE

1 TEASPOON GRENADINE

CLUB SODA

LIME PEEL STRIPS AND MARASCHINO
CHERRIES, TO GARNISH

SINGAPORE SLING

1. Put cracked ice into a cocktail shaker and pour the gin over it.

2. Pour in the cherry brandy, lemon juice, and grenadine and shake vigorously until well frosted.

3. Fill a chilled glass halfway with cracked ice and strain the cocktail over the ice.

4. Top off with club soda and garnish with the lime peel and cherries. Serve immediately.

SERVES 1

TOM COLLINS

1. Put cracked ice into a cocktail shaker.

2. Pour the gin, lemon juice, and sugar syrup over the ice and shake vigorously until well frosted.

3. Strain into a chilled Collins glass.

4. Top off with club soda and garnish with the lemon slices. Serve immediately.

INGREDIENTS

2½ OUNCES GIN

1¾ OUNCES LEMON JUICE

½ OUNCE SUGAR SYRUP

CLUB SODA

LEMON SLICES,
TO GARNISH

SERVES 1

BELLE COLLINS

1. Muddle the mint sprigs.

2. Place the mint in a chilled old-fashioned glass and pour in the gin, lemon juice, and sugar syrup.

3. Add the crushed ice to the glass.

4. Top off with sparkling water, stir gently, and garnish with more fresh mint. Serve immediately.

INGREDIENTS

2 FRESH MINT SPRIGS, PLUS
EXTRA TO GARNISH

1¾ OUNCES GIN

¾ OUNCE LEMON JUICE

1 TEASPOON SUGAR SYRUP

4-6 ICE CUBES, CRUSHED

SPARKLING WATER

GIN RICKEY

SERVES 1

INGREDIENTS

CRACKED ICE

1¾ OUNCES GIN

¾ OUNCE LIME JUICE

CLUB SODA

LEMON SLICE,
TO GARNISH

1. Fill a chilled highball glass or goblet with cracked ice.

2. Pour the gin and lime juice over the ice.

3. Top off with club soda.

4. Stir gently to mix and garnish with a lemon slice. Serve immediately.

A SLOE KISS

SERVES 1

INGREDIENTS

½ OUNCE SLOE GIN

½ OUNCE SOUTHERN COMFORT

¾ OUNCE VODKA

1 TEASPOON AMARETTO

CRACKED ICE

SPLASH GALLIANO

ORANGE JUICE

ORANGE PEEL TWIST,
TO GARNISH

1. Put cracked ice into a cocktail shaker, pour the sloe gin, Southern Comfort, vodka, and amaretto over the ice, and shake until well frosted.

2. Strain into a long, chilled glass filled with cracked ice.

3. Splash on the Galliano.

4. Top off with orange juice and garnish with the orange peel. Serve immediately.

SERVES 1

INGREDIENTS

¾ OUNCE GIN

¾ OUNCE WHITE RUM

¾ OUNCE PINEAPPLE JUICE

PALM BEACH

1. Shake the gin, rum, and pineapple juice vigorously over cracked ice until well frosted.

2. Strain into a chilled glass.

SERVES 1

INGREDIENTS

¾ OUNCE GIN

½ OUNCE TEQUILA

½ OUNCE DRY ORANGE CURAÇAO

½ OUNCE LEMON JUICE

DASH EGG WHITE

ORANGE PEEL, TO GARNISH

FIREFLY

1. Shake all the liquid ingredients well over ice until frosted.

2. Strain into a chilled cocktail glass and garnish with a twist of orange peel. Serve immediately.

GIN SLING

SERVES 1

1. Place the sugar in an old-fashioned glass and add 4 ounces of hot water. Stir until the sugar is dissolved.

2. Stir in the gin, sprinkle with nutmeg, and serve immediately with a slice of lemon.

INGREDIENTS

1 SUGAR CUBE

¾ OUNCE GIN

FRESHLY GRATED NUTMEG

LEMON SLICE, TO SERVE

MAIDEN'S PRAYER

SERVES 1

1. Shake the ingredients vigorously over ice until well frosted.

2. Strain into a chilled cocktail glass and garnish with the twist of lemon peel. Serve immediately.

INGREDIENTS

¾ OUNCE GIN

¾ OUNCE TRIPLE SEC

1 TEASPOON ORANGE JUICE

1 TEASPOON LEMON JUICE

LEMON PEEL TWIST, TO GARNISH

SERVES 1

INGREDIENTS

2 ½ OUNCES GIN

¾ OUNCE LEMON JUICE

½ OUNCE GRENADINE

1 TEASPOON SUGAR SYRUP

CLUB SODA

ORANGE WEDGE, TO GARNISH

DAISY

1. Put cracked ice into a cocktail shaker.

2. Pour the gin, lemon juice, grenadine, and sugar syrup over the ice and shake vigorously until well frosted.

3. Strain the cocktail into a chilled highball glass.

4. Top off with club soda, stir gently, and garnish with the orange wedge. Serve immediately.

BLOODHOUND

1. Put the gin, sweet vermouth, dry vermouth, and strawberries into a blender.

2. Add the cracked ice.

3. Blend until smooth.

4. Pour into a chilled cocktail glass and garnish with the remaining strawberry. Serve immediately.

SERVES 1

INGREDIENTS

1³/₄ OUNCES GIN

¾ OUNCE SWEET VERMOUTH

¾ OUNCE DRY VERMOUTH

3 STRAWBERRIES,
PLUS ONE TO GARNISH

4–6 ICE CUBES, CRACKED

ALASKA

1. Shake the gin and Chartreuse over ice cubes until well frosted.

2. Strain into a chilled glass and serve immediately.

SERVES 1

INGREDIENTS

½ OUNCE GIN

½ OUNCE YELLOW CHARTREUSE

HAWAIIAN
ORANGE BLOSSOM

1. Shake the liquid ingredients vigorously over ice until well frosted.

2. Strain into a chilled wine glass and serve immediately, garnished with pineapple slices and leaves.

SERVES 1

INGREDIENTS

1¾ OUNCES GIN

¾ OUNCE TRIPLE SEC

1¾ OUNCES ORANGE JUICE

¾ OUNCE PINEAPPLE JUICE

ICE

PINEAPPLE SLICES
AND LEAVES, TO GARNISH

WEDDING BELLE

1. Shake the liquid ingredients over ice cubes until well frosted.

2. Strain into a chilled glass and serve immediately garnished with a twist of orange peel.

INGREDIENTS

1¾ OUNCES GIN

1 ¾ OUNCES DUBONNET

¾ OUNCE CHERRY BRANDY

¾ OUNCE ORANGE JUICE

ORANGE PEEL, TO GARNISH

BRIDE'S MOTHER

1. Shake the liquid ingredients vigorously over ice cubes until well frosted.

2. Strain over crushed ice and garnish with grapefruit slices. Serve immediately.

INGREDIENTS

1¼ OUNCES SLOE GIN

¾ OUNCE GIN

2 OUNCES GRAPEFRUIT JUICE

½ OUNCE SUGAR SYRUP

CRUSHED ICE

GRAPEFRUIT SLICES, TO GARNISH

SERVES 4

INGREDIENTS

2½ OUNCES GRAPEFRUIT JUICE

3½ OUNCES GIN

¾ OUNCE KIRSCH

3½ OUNCES WHITE WINE

½ TEASPOON LEMON ZEST

MOONLIGHT

1. Shake all the ingredients vigorously over ice cubes until well frosted. Strain into chilled glasses and serve immediately.

BARTENDER'S TIP

This light cocktail is ideal to make for several people at once.

SERVES 1

INGREDIENTS

1¾ OUNCES GIN

½ OUNCE MARASCHINO

½ OUNCE GRAPEFRUIT JUICE

FRESH MINT SPRIGS, TO GARNISH

SEVENTH HEAVEN

1. Shake all the liquid ingredients vigorously over ice cubes until well frosted.

2. Strain into a chilled cocktail glass. Garnish with fresh mint and serve immediately.

SERVES 1

INGREDIENTS

¾ OUNCE GIN

1¾ OUNCES APRICOT NECTAR OR PEACH NECTAR

¾ OUNCE LIGHT CREAM

CRUSHED ICE

½ OUNCE STRAWBERRY SYRUP

FRESH STRAWBERRY AND PEACH SLICES, TO GARNISH

TEARDROP

1. Put the gin, apricot nectar, and cream into a blender and blend for 5-10 seconds, until thick and frothy.

2. Pour into a long glass filled with crushed ice.

3. Splash the strawberry syrup on the top and garnish with the strawberry and peach slices. Serve immediately.

SERVES 1

INGREDIENTS

¾ OUNCE GIN

¾ OUNCE PASSION FRUIT NECTAR

4 CUBES MELON OR MANGO

4–6 ICE CUBES, CRACKED, PLUS EXTRA TO FILL THE GLASS

1-2 TEASPOONS BLUE CURAÇAO

BLUE BLOODED

1. Put the gin, passion fruit nectar, melon cubes, and cracked ice into a blender and blend until smooth and frosted.

2. Pour into a tall, chilled glass filled with cracked ice and top off with the curaçao. Serve immediately.

PUSSYCAT

1. Fill a chilled old-fashioned glass halfway with cracked ice.

2. Dash the grenadine over the ice and add the gin.

3. Top off with pineapple juice and garnish with the pineapple slice. Serve immediately.

SERVES 1

INGREDIENTS

CRACKED ICE

DASH GRENADINE

1¾ OUNCES GIN

PINEAPPLE JUICE

PINEAPPLE SLICE, TO GARNISH

BLEU BLEU BLEU

1. Put crushed ice into a cocktail shaker.

2. Add the gin, vodka, tequila, lemon juice, egg white, and curaçao and shake until frosted.

3. Strain the cocktail into a tall glass filled with crushed ice and top off with club soda. Garnish with a lemon slice. Serve immediately.

SERVES 1

INGREDIENTS

CRUSHED ICE

¾ OUNCE GIN

¾ OUNCE VODKA

¾ OUNCE TEQUILA

¼ OUNCE FRESH LEMON JUICE

2 DASHES EGG WHITE

¾ OUNCE BLUE CURAÇAO

CLUB SODA

LEMON SLICE, TO GARNISH

SERVES 1

INGREDIENTS

1¾ OUNCES GIN

¾ OUNCE LEMON JUICE

¾ OUNCE GRENADINE

1 EGG WHITE

LIME PEEL TWIST,
TO GARNISH

GRAND ROYAL CLOVER CLUB

1. Pour the first four ingredients over ice.

2. Shake vigorously until well frosted and strain into a chilled cocktail glass.

3. Garnish with a twist of lime peel and serve immediately.

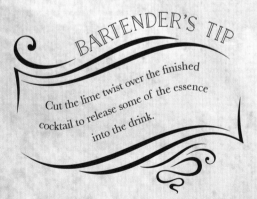

BARTENDER'S TIP

Cut the lime twist over the finished cocktail to release some of the essence into the drink.

THE BLUE TRAIN

SERVES 1

INGREDIENTS

1¾ OUNCES GIN

¾ OUNCE TRIPLE SEC

¾ OUNCE LEMON JUICE

SPLASH BLUE CURAÇAO

1. Pour all of the liquid ingredients into a cocktail shaker filled with cracked ice.

2. Shake vigorously until frosted and strain into a chilled cocktail glass. Serve immediately.

SERVES 1

SAKETINI

1. Shake the gin and sake vigorously over ice until well frosted.

2. Strain into a chilled cocktail glass and garnish with a twist of lemon peel. Serve immediately.

INGREDIENTS

2½ OUNCES GIN

½ MEASURE SAKE

LEMON PEEL TWIST, TO GARNISH

SERVES 1

GREEN LADY

1. Shake the ingredients vigorously over ice until well frosted.

2. Strain into a chilled cocktail glass and serve immediately.

INGREDIENTS

1¾ OUNCES GIN

¾ OUNCE GREEN CHARTREUSE

DASH LIME JUICE

SERVES 1

INGREDIENTS

1¾ OUNCES GIN

1 TEASPOON GRENADINE

1 EGG WHITE

DASH ORANGE BITTERS

BACHELOR'S BAIT

1. Shake the gin, grenadine, and egg white together over ice cubes until well frosted.

2. Add a dash of orange bitters, give the mixture another quick shake, and strain into a chilled cocktail glass. Serve immediately.

SERVES 1

INGREDIENTS

1¾ OUNCES GIN

1¼ OUNCES MADEIRA OR SHERRY

1 TEASPOON GRENADINE

MARASCHINO CHERRIES, TO GARNISH

CREOLE LADY

1. Pour the liquid ingredients over cracked ice in a mixing glass.

2. Stir well to mix, then strain into a chilled glass.

3. Garnish with the maraschino cherries and serve immediately.

SERVES 1

INGREDIENTS

1¾ OUNCES VODKA

¾ OUNCE TRIPLE SEC

¾ OUNCE LIME JUICE

⅞ OUNCE CRANBERRY JUICE

ORANGE PEEL STRIP, TO GARNISH

COSMOPOLITAN

1. Put cracked ice into a cocktail shaker.

2. Pour the liquid ingredients over the ice.

3. Shake vigorously until well frosted.

4. Strain into a chilled cocktail glass and garnish with the orange peel. Serve immediately.

WOO-WOO

1. Fill a chilled cocktail glass halfway with crushed ice.

2. Pour the cranberry juice over the ice.

3. Add the vodka and peach schnapps.

4. Stir well to mix and serve.

SERVES 1

INGREDIENTS

CRUSHED ICE

3½ OUNCES CRANBERRY JUICE

1¾ OUNCES VODKA

1¾ OUNCES PEACH SCHNAPPS

SEX ON THE BEACH

1. Put crushed ice into a cocktail shaker and pour over the peach schnapps, vodka, orange juice, and cranberry juice.

2. Shake until well frosted and strain into a glass filled with ice.

3. Squeeze the lemon juice over the top and garnish with the orange peel. Serve immediately.

INGREDIENTS

¾ OUNCE PEACH SCHNAPPS

¾ OUNCE VODKA

1¾ OUNCES FRESH ORANGE JUICE

2½ OUNCES CRANBERRY OR PEACH JUICE

CRUSHED ICE

DASH LEMON JUICE

ORANGE PEEL TWIST, TO GARNISH

FUZZY NAVEL

1. Put cracked ice into a cocktail shaker.

2. Pour the liquid ingredients over the ice and shake vigorously until well frosted.

3. Strain into chilled cocktail glasses. Serve immediately.

INGREDIENTS

1¾ OUNCES VODKA

¾ OUNCE PEACH SCHNAPPS

1 CUP ORANGE JUICE

SALTY DOG

1. Mix the sugar and salt in a saucer. Rub the rim of a chilled cocktail glass with the lime wedge and dip into the sugar-and-salt mixture to coat.

2. Fill the glass with cracked ice and pour the vodka over the ice.

3. Top off with the grapefruit juice and stir. Serve immediately.

INGREDIENTS

1 TABLESPOON GRANULATED SUGAR

1 TABLESPOON KOSHER SALT

1 LIME WEDGE

CRACKED ICE

1¼ OUNCES VODKA

GRAPEFRUIT JUICE

KAMIKAZE

1. Put cracked ice into a cocktail shaker.

2. Pour the vodka, triple sec, lime juice, and lemon juice over the ice and shake until well frosted.

3. Strain into a chilled glass.

4. Top off with wine and garnish with the cucumber and lime slices. Serve immediately.

INGREDIENTS

¾ OUNCE VODKA

¾ OUNCE TRIPLE SEC

½ OUNCE FRESH LIME JUICE

½ OUNCE FRESH LEMON JUICE

DRY WHITE WINE, CHILLED

CUCUMBER AND LIME SLICES, TO GARNISH

SERVES 1

INGREDIENTS

CRACKED ICE

2¼ OUNCES VODKA

7 OUNCES ORANGE JUICE

2 TEASPOONS GALLIANO

**MARASCHINO CHERRY
AND ORANGE SLICE,
TO GARNISH**

HARVEY WALLBANGER

1. Fill a tall glass halfway with cracked ice.

2. Pour the vodka and orange juice over the ice.

3. Float the Galliano on top.

4. Garnish with the cherry and the orange slice. Serve immediately.

PEARTINI

SERVES 1

INGREDIENTS

1 TEASPOON SUPERFINE SUGAR
PINCH GROUND CINNAMON
1 LEMON WEDGE
¼ OUNCE VODKA
¾ OUNCE PEAR BRANDY

1. Mix the sugar and cinnamon in a saucer.

2. Rub the rim of a cocktail glass with the lemon wedge.

3. Dip into the sugar-and-cinnamon mixture to coat.

4. Put cracked ice into a cocktail shaker and pour in the vodka and pear brandy. Shake well and strain into the glass. Serve immediately.

SERVES 1

BLACK BEAUTY

1. Stir the vodka and Sambuca with ice in a mixing glass until frosted.

2. Strain into a chilled cocktail glass and garnish with the olive. Serve immediately.

INGREDIENTS

1¾ OUNCES VODKA

¾ OUNCE BLACK SAMBUCA

BLACK RIPE OLIVE, TO GARNISH

SERVES 1

SPOTTED BIKINI

1. Scoop the passion fruit flesh into a bowl. Shake the liquid ingredients over ice until well frosted.

2. Strain into a chilled cocktail glass and add the passion fruit at the last minute.

3. Garnish with a slice of lemon peel and serve immediately.

INGREDIENTS

1 RIPE PASSION FRUIT

1¾ OUNCES VODKA

¾ OUNCE WHITE RUM

¾ OUNCE COLD MILK

JUICE OF ½ LEMON

SLICE OF LEMON PEEL, TO GARNISH

SERVES 1

INGREDIENTS

ORANGE WEDGES
SUPERFINE SUGAR
1¾ OUNCES VODKA, CHILLED

CORDLESS SCREWDRIVER

1. Rub the rim of a chilled shot glass with an orange wedge, then dip into a saucer of sugar to frost.

2. Pour the vodka into the glass.

3. Dip an orange wedge into the sugar.

4. Down the vodka in one go and suck the orange.

SERVES 1

INGREDIENTS

¾ OUNCE VODKA
½ OUNCE COINTREAU
½ OUNCE BLUE CURAÇAO

BLUE MONDAY

1. Put cracked ice into a mixing glass or pitcher and pour in the vodka, Cointreau, and curaçao.

2. Stir well, strain into a cocktail glass, and serve immediately.

SERVES 1

INGREDIENTS

DASH HOT PEPPER SAUCE

DASH WORCESTERSHIRE
SAUCE

1¾ OUNCES VODKA

5¼ OUNCES TOMATO JUICE

JUICE OF ½ LEMON

PINCH CELERY SALT

PINCH CAYENNE PEPPER

CELERY STALK AND LEMON SLICE,
TO GARNISH

BLOODY MARY

1. Put cracked ice into a cocktail shaker. Dash the hot pepper sauce and Worcestershire sauce over the ice.

2. Add the vodka, tomato juice, and lemon juice and shake vigorously until well frosted.

3. Strain into a tall, chilled glass, add the celery salt and cayenne pepper, and garnish with the celery stalk and lemon slice. Serve immediately.

BARTENDER'S TIP

To make the Canadian favorite Bloody Caesar, simply replace the tomato juice with clamato juice. You can find clamato juice in supermarkets.

LONG ISLAND ICED TEA

1. Put cracked ice into a cocktail shaker. Pour all the liquid ingredients except the cola over the ice, add the sugar, and shake vigorously until well frosted.

2. Fill a tall glass with cracked ice and strain over the cocktail.

3. Top off with cola, garnish with the lime wedge, and serve immediately.

SERVES 1

INGREDIENTS

¾ OUNCE VODKA

¾ OUNCE GIN

¾ OUNCE WHITE TEQUILA

¾ OUNCE WHITE RUM

½ OUNCE WHITE CRÈME DE MENTHE

1¾ OUNCES LEMON JUICE

1 TEASPOON SUPERFINE SUGAR

CRACKED ICE

COLA

LIME WEDGE, TO GARNISH

SERVES 1

FLYING GRASSHOPPER

INGREDIENTS

4-6 ICE CUBES, CRACKED

¾ OUNCE VODKA

¾ OUNCE GREEN CRÈME DE MENTHE

¾ OUNCE CRÈME DE CACAO

FRESH MINT, TO GARNISH

1. Put the cracked ice into a mixing glass.

2. Pour the vodka, crème de menthe, and crème de cacao over the ice and stir well.

3. Strain into a chilled cocktail glass and garnish with a sprig of fresh mint. Serve immediately.

SERVES 1

AURORA BOREALIS

INGREDIENTS

¾ OUNCE CHILLED GRAPPA OR VODKA

¾ OUNCE CHILLED GREEN CHARTREUSE

½ OUNCE CHILLED ORANGE CURAÇAO

FEW DROPS CHILLED CRÈME DE CASSIS

1. Pour the grappa slowly over the back of a spoon around one side of a well chilled shot glass.

2. Gently pour the Chartreuse around the other side.

3. Pour the curaçao gently into the middle.

4. Add a few drops of crème de cassis. Serve immediately.

LAST MANGO IN PARIS

INGREDIENTS

1¾ OUNCES VODKA

¾ OUNCE FRAMBOISE

¾ OUNCE LIME JUICE

½ MANGO, PEELED, PITTED, AND CHOPPED

2 HALVED STRAWBERRIES

LIME SLICE, TO GARNISH

1. Mix the ingredients in a blender until slushy.

2. Pour into a chilled glass and garnish with a slice of lime. Serve immediately.

SERVES 1

THUNDERBIRD

1. Pour the vodka into a frosted cocktail glass.

2. Add the other ingredients slowly and stir only once. Serve immediately.

INGREDIENTS

1¾ OUNCES ICED VODKA

DASH PARFAIT AMOUR (AVAILABLE FROM SPECIALTY COCKTAIL SUPPLIERS)

DASH CASSIS

SMALL PIECE OF ORANGE ZEST

1 ROSE OR VIOLET PETAL

SERVES 1

INGREDIENTS

1¾ OUNCES VODKA

½ OUNCE CREAM OF COCONUT

1¾ OUNCES PINEAPPLE JUICE

4–6 ICE CUBES, CRUSHED

FRESH PINEAPPLE SLICE, TO GARNISH

MIMI

1. Put the vodka, cream of coconut, pineapple juice, and crushed ice into a blender.

2. Blend for a few seconds until frothy.

3. Pour into a chilled cocktail glass.

4. Garnish with a slice of pineapple. Serve immediately.

SUNNY BAY

1. Pour the ingredients into a shaker filled with ice.

2. Shake well.

3. Strain into a chilled cocktail glass and garnish with the cherry on a toothpick. Serve immediately.

SERVES 1

INGREDIENTS

1¼ OUNCES VODKA

½ OUNCE MELON LIQUEUR

1¾ OUNCES PINEAPPLE JUICE

MARASCHINO CHERRY, TO GARNISH

SERVES 1

INGREDIENTS

1¼ OUNCES VODKA

½ OUNCE CRANBERRY JUICE

PINK GRAPEFRUIT JUICE

SEA BREEZE

1. Put cracked ice into a cocktail shaker.

2. Pour the vodka and cranberry juice over the ice and shake until frosted.

3. Strain into a chilled tumbler and top off with pink grapefruit juice. Serve immediately.

SERVES 1

INGREDIENTS

1¼ OUNCES VODKA

¾ OUNCE ELDERFLOWER SYRUP (CORDIAL)

2½ OUNCES CRANBERRY JUICE

CRACKED ICE

CLUB SODA

LIME SLICE AND LIME PEEL TWIST, TO GARNISH

CRANBERRY COLLINS

1. Put cracked ice into a cocktail shaker.

2. Pour the vodka, elderflower syrup, and cranberry juice over the ice and shake until well frosted.

3. Strain into a Collins glass filled with cracked ice.

4. Top off with club soda and garnish with the lime slice and peel. Serve immediately.

SERVES 1

MOSCOW MULE

1. Put cracked ice into a cocktail shaker.

2. Pour the vodka and lime juice over the ice and shake vigorously until well frosted.

3. Fill a chilled glass halfway with cracked ice and strain over the cocktail.

4. Top off with ginger beer and garnish with the lime wedge. Serve immediately.

INGREDIENTS

1¼ OUNCES VODKA

¾ OUNCE LIME JUICE

CRACKED ICE

GINGER BEER

LIME WEDGE, TO GARNISH

SERVES 1

SCREWDRIVER

1. Fill a chilled glass with cracked ice. Pour the vodka over the ice.

2. Top off with orange juice and stir well to mix.

3. Garnish with the orange slice. Serve immediately.

INGREDIENTS

CRACKED ICE

1¼ OUNCES VODKA

ORANGE JUICE

ORANGE SLICE, TO GARNISH

METROPOLITAN

1. Rub the rim of a cocktail glass with the lemon wedge.

2. Dip into the sugar to coat.

3. Put cracked ice cubes into a cocktail shaker and pour the liquid ingredients over the ice.

4. Cover and shake vigorously until well frosted. Strain into the glass and serve immediately.

SERVES 1

INGREDIENTS

1 LEMON WEDGE

1 TABLESPOON SUPERFINE SUGAR

½ OUNCE VODKA

½ OUNCE FRAMBOISE LIQUEUR

½ OUNCE CRANBERRY JUICE

½ OUNCE ORANGE JUICE

VODKA ESPRESSO

1. Put cracked ice into a cocktail shaker.

2. Pour in the coffee and vodka, add the sugar, and shake vigorously until well frosted.

3. Strain into a chilled cocktail glass.

4. Float the Amarula on top. Serve immediately.

SERVES 1

INGREDIENTS

1¾ OUNCES ESPRESSO OR OTHER STRONG BLACK COFFEE, COOLED

¾ OUNCE VODKA

2 TEASPOONS SUPERFINE SUGAR

¼ OUNCE AMARULA

RUM, WHISKIES & BRANDY

SERVES 1

DAIQUIRI

1. Put cracked ice into a cocktail shaker.

2. Pour the rum, sugar water, and lime juice over the ice. Shake vigorously until well frosted.

3. Strain into a chilled cocktail glass and garnish with a wedge of lime. Serve immediately.

INGREDIENTS

1¾ OUNCES WHITE RUM

½ TEASPOON SUPERFINE SUGAR, DISSOLVED IN 1 TABLESPOON BOILING WATER

1½ TEASPOONS LIME JUICE

LIME WEDGE, TO GARNISH

SERVES 1

BANANA COLADA

1. Blend the crushed ice in a blender with the white rum, pineapple juice, Malibu, and sliced banana.

2. Blend until smooth, then pour, without straining, into a chilled highball glass and serve immediately with pineapple wedges and a straw.

INGREDIENTS

4-6 ICE CUBES, CRUSHED

1¾ OUNCES WHITE RUM

3½ OUNCES PINEAPPLE JUICE

¾ OUNCE MALIBU

1 BANANA, PEELED AND SLICED

PINEAPPLE WEDGES

SERVES 1

HURRICANE

1. Put cracked ice into a cocktail shaker.

2. Add the rum, lemon juice, and orange and passion fruit juice, and shake until well combined.

3. Pour the cocktail into a tall, chilled glass and top off with club soda.

4. Garnish with the orange slices and cherries and serve immediately.

INGREDIENTS

3½ OUNCES DARK RUM

¾ OUNCE LEMON JUICE

1¾ OUNCES ORANGE AND PASSION FRUIT JUICE

CLUB SODA

ORANGE SLICES AND MARASCHINO CHERRIES, TO GARNISH

SERVES 1

STRAWBERRY COLADA

1. Put the crushed ice into a blender. Add the rum, pineapple juice, and cream of coconut.

2. Hull the strawberries and add to the blender. Blend until smooth, then pour, without straining, into a tall, chilled glass.

3. Garnish with the pineapple wedge and strawberry and serve immediately.

INGREDIENTS

4-6 ICE CUBES, CRUSHED

2½ OUNCES GOLDEN RUM

3½ OUNCES PINEAPPLE JUICE

¾ OUNCE CREAM OF COCONUT

6 STRAWBERRIES

PINEAPPLE WEDGE AND HALVED STRAWBERRY, TO GARNISH

INGREDIENTS

4-6 ICE CUBES, CRUSHED

1¾ OUNCES WHITE RUM

¾ OUNCE DARK RUM

2½ OUNCES PINEAPPLE JUICE

1¾ OUNCES CREAM OF COCONUT

MARASCHINO CHERRY AND PINEAPPLE WEDGE, TO GARNISH

PIÑA COLADA

1. Put the crushed ice into a blender. Pour the white rum, dark rum, and pineapple juice over the ice.

2. Add the cream of coconut to the blender and blend until smooth.

3. Pour, without straining, into a chilled glass.

4. Garnish with the maraschino cherry and pineapple wedge.

5. Serve immediately.

CLUB MOJITO

SERVES 1

INGREDIENTS

1 TEASPOON SUGAR SYRUP

6 FRESH MINT LEAVES, PLUS EXTRA TO GARNISH

JUICE OF ½ LIME

4–6 ICE CUBES, CRACKED

1¼ OUNCES JAMAICAN RUM

CLUB SODA

DASH ANGOSTURA BITTERS

1. Put the sugar syrup, mint leaves, and lime juice into an old-fashioned glass.

2. Muddle the mint leaves, then add the cracked ice and the rum.

3. Top off with club soda.

4. Finish with the Angostura bitters and garnish with the remaining mint leaves.

5. Serve immediately.

SERVES 1

INGREDIENTS

¾ OUNCE WHITE RUM

¾ OUNCE MANDARINE BRANDY
OR GRAND MARNIER

¾ OUNCE FRESH ORANGE JUICE

¾ OUNCE PINEAPPLE JUICE

SPLASH GRENADINE

FRESH PINEAPPLE SLICE AND
MARASCHINO CHERRY, TO GARNISH

BAJAN SUN

1. Put crushed ice into a cocktail shaker.

2. Pour the rum, brandy, orange juice, and pineapple juice over the ice.

3. Add the grenadine and shake vigorously.

4. Strain into a tall, chilled glass and garnish with the pineapple slice and maraschino cherry. Serve immediately.

SERVES 1

INGREDIENTS

1¾ OUNCES DARK RUM

¾ OUNCE SOUTHERN COMFORT

¾ OUNCE LEMON JUICE

1 TEASPOON BROWN SUGAR

SPARKLING WATER

1 TEASPOON RUBY PORT

PLANTATION PUNCH

1. Put cracked ice cubes into a cocktail shaker. Add the rum, Southern Comfort, lemon juice, and brown sugar.

2. Shake vigorously until well frosted. Strain into a tall, chilled glass. Top off with sparkling water.

3. Float the port on top by pouring it gently over the back of a teaspoon. Serve immediately.

OCEAN BREEZE

1. Put crushed ice into a cocktail shaker.

2. Pour the white rum, amaretto, blue curaçao, and pineapple juice over the ice and shake well.

3. Strain into a tall, chilled glass and top off with club soda. Serve immediately.

INGREDIENTS

¾ OUNCE WHITE RUM

¾ OUNCE AMARETTO

½ OUNCE BLUE CURAÇAO

½ OUNCE PINEAPPLE JUICE

CLUB SODA

BLUE HAWAIIAN

1. Put crushed ice in a cocktail shaker.

2. Pour the liquid ingredients over the ice. Shake vigorously until well frosted and strain into a chilled wine glass.

3. Garnish with the pineapple wedge. Serve immediately.

INGREDIENTS

1¾ OUNCES BACARDI RUM

½ OUNCE BLUE CURAÇAO

¾ OUNCE PINEAPPLE JUICE

½ OUNCE CREAM OF COCONUT

PINEAPPLE WEDGE, TO GARNISH

MAI TAI

SERVES 1

INGREDIENTS

¾ OUNCE WHITE RUM

¾ OUNCE DARK RUM

¾ OUNCE ORANGE CURAÇAO

¼ OUNCE LIME JUICE

¾ OUNCE ORGEAT SYRUP

½ OUNCE GRENADINE

TO GARNISH

PINEAPPLE WEDGE

PINEAPPLE LEAVES

MARASCHINO CHERRY

ORANGE PEEL TWIST

1. Put cracked ice into a cocktail shaker. Pour the white rum, dark rum, curaçao, lime juice, orgeat syrup, and grenadine over the ice.

2. Shake vigorously until well frosted and strain into a chilled glass.

3. Garnish with the pineapple wedge, leaves, cherry, and orange peel. Serve immediately.

SERVES 3

INGREDIENTS

1¼ OUNCES DARK RUM

1¾ OUNCES WHITE RUM

¾ OUNCE GOLDEN RUM

¼ OUNCE TRIPLE SEC

3/4 OUNCE LIME JUICE

¾ OUNCE ORANGE JUICE

¾ OUNCE PINEAPPLE JUICE

¾ OUNCE GUAVA JUICE

½ OUNCE GRENADINE

½ OUNCE ORGEAT SYRUP

1 TEASPOON PERNOD

FRESH MINT SPRIGS
AND PINEAPPLE WEDGES,
TO GARNISH

ZOMBIE

1. Put crushed ice into a cocktail shaker.

2. Pour the liquid ingredients over the ice and shake vigorously until well frosted.

3. Pour the cocktail into chilled glasses and garnish with the fresh mint and the pineapple wedges. Serve immediately.

CUBA LIBRE

SERVES 1

INGREDIENTS

CRACKED ICE

1¾ OUNCES WHITE RUM

COLA

LIME WEDGE, TO GARNISH

1. Fill a highball glass halfway with cracked ice.

2. Pour the rum over the ice and top off with cola.

3. Stir gently to mix and garnish with the lime wedge. Serve immediately.

CUBAN SPECIAL

SERVES 1

INGREDIENTS

1¾ OUNCES WHITE RUM

¾ OUNCE LIME JUICE

½ OUNCE PINEAPPLE JUICE

1 TEASPOON TRIPLE SEC

PINEAPPLE WEDGES, TO GARNISH

1. Put cracked ice cubes into a cocktail shaker.

2. Pour the rum, lime juice, pineapple juice, and triple sec over the ice. Shake vigorously until well frosted. Strain into a chilled cocktail glass.

3. Garnish with the pineapple wedges and serve immediately.

SERVES 8

INGREDIENTS

6 EGGS

4–5 TEASPOONS CONFECTIONERS' SUGAR

FRESHLY GRATED NUTMEG, PLUS EXTRA FOR SPRINKLING

16 OUNCES (2 CUPS) DARK RUM

5 CUPS MILK, WARMED

RUM NOGGIN

1. Whisk the eggs in a punch bowl with the sugar and a little nutmeg.

2. Whisk in the rum and gradually stir in the milk.

3. Warm through gently, if desired, and serve immediately in small heatproof glasses or mugs, sprinkled with nutmeg.

SERVES 1

INGREDIENTS

1 TEASPOON CONFECTIONERS' SUGAR

1¾ OUNCES SPARKLING WATER

CRACKED ICE

1¾ OUNCES WHITE RUM

LIME SLICE AND ORANGE SLICE, TO GARNISH

RUM COBBLER

1. Put the sugar into a chilled glass. Add the sparkling water and stir until the sugar has dissolved.

2. Fill the glass with cracked ice and pour in the rum. Stir well and garnish with a lime slice and an orange slice. Serve immediately.

FROZEN PEACH DAIQUIRI

1. Put the crushed ice and the peach into a blender.

2. Add the rum, lime juice, and sugar syrup and blend until slushy.

3. Pour into a chilled cocktail glass.

4. Garnish with the peach slice.

5. Serve immediately.

SERVES 1

INGREDIENTS

6 CRUSHED ICE CUBES

½ PEACH, CHOPPED

1¾ OUNCES WHITE RUM

¾ OUNCE LIME JUICE

1 TEASPOON SUGAR SYRUP

PEACH SLICE, TO GARNISH

RUM COOLER

SERVES 1

INGREDIENTS

CRACKED ICE

1¼ OUNCES WHITE RUM

1¼ OUNCES PINEAPPLE JUICE

1 BANANA, PEELED AND SLICED

JUICE OF 1 LIME

LIME PEEL TWIST, TO GARNISH

1. Put the cracked ice, rum, pineapple juice, and banana into a blender.

2. Add the lime juice and blend for about 1 minute or until smooth.

3. Fill a chilled glass with cracked ice and pour the cocktail over the ice.

4. Garnish with the lime peel.

5. Serve immediately.

SERVES 1

WHISKEY SOUR

1. Put cracked ice cubes into a cocktail shaker and pour whiskey over the ice.

2. Add the lime juice and sugar and shake well.

3. Strain into a cocktail glass and garnish with the slice of lime and a cherry. Serve immediately.

INGREDIENTS

1¼ OUNCES BLENDED WHISKEY

¾ OUNCE LIME JUICE

1 TEASPOON CONFECTIONERS' SUGAR
OR SUGAR SYRUP

LIME SLICE AND
MARASCHINO CHERRY,
TO GARNISH

SERVES 1

WHISKEY RICKEY

1. Put crushed ice into a chilled highball glass.

2. Pour the whiskey and lime juice over the ice and top with club soda.

3. Stir gently to mix, garnish with the lime slice, and serve immediately.

INGREDIENTS

1¼ OUNCES BLENDED WHISKEY

¾ OUNCE LIME JUICE

CLUB SODA

LIME SLICE, TO GARNISH

SERVES 1

HIGHLAND FLING

1. Put cracked ice into a mixing glass.

2. Pour the Angostura bitters over the ice. Pour in the whisky and vermouth and stir well to mix.

3. Strain into a chilled glass and garnish with the olive. Serve immediately.

INGREDIENTS

DASH ANGOSTURA BITTERS

1¾ OUNCES SCOTCH WHISKY

¾ OUNCE SWEET VERMOUTH

COCKTAIL OLIVE, TO GARNISH

SERVES 1

WHISKEY SLING

1. Put the sugar into a mixing glass.

2. Add the lemon juice and water and stir until the sugar has dissolved.

3. Pour in the whiskey and stir to mix.

4. Fill a chilled old-fashioned glass with cracked ice and strain the cocktail over it.

5. Garnish with the orange wedge and serve immediately.

INGREDIENTS

1 TEASPOON CONFECTIONERS' SUGAR

¾ OUNCE LEMON JUICE

1 TEASPOON WATER

1¾ OUNCES BLENDED WHISKEY

CRACKED ICE

ORANGE WEDGE, TO GARNISH

SERVES 1

INGREDIENTS

1¼ OUNCES SCOTCH WHISKY

1¼ OUNCES DRY VERMOUTH

1¾ OUNCES PINK GRAPEFRUIT JUICE

**ORANGE PEEL STRIP,
TO GARNISH**

MIAMI BEACH

1. Put cracked ice into a cocktail shaker.

2. Pour the whisky, vermouth, and grapefruit juice over the ice.

3. Shake vigorously until well frosted. Strain into a chilled cocktail glass.

4. Garnish with the orange peel strip and serve immediately.

BOSTON SOUR

1. Put cracked ice into a cocktail shaker.

2. Pour the lemon juice, whiskey, and sugar syrup over the ice.

3. Add the egg white.

4. Shake until chilled. Strain into a cocktail glass and garnish with the lemon slice and a maraschino cherry. Serve immediately.

SERVES 1

INGREDIENTS

¾ OUNCE LEMON JUICE OR LIME JUICE

1¾ OUNCES BLENDED WHISKEY

1 TEASPOON SUGAR SYRUP

1 EGG WHITE

LEMON SLICE AND MARASCHINO CHERRY, TO GARNISH

SERVES 1

KLONDIKE COOLER

1. Put the sugar into a chilled glass and add the ginger ale. Stir until the sugar has dissolved.

2. Fill the glass with cracked ice. Pour the whiskey over the ice.

3. Top off with sparkling water. Stir gently and garnish with the lemon peel. Serve immediately.

INGREDIENTS

½ TEASPOON CONFECTIONERS' SUGAR

¾ OUNCE GINGER ALE

CRACKED ICE

1¾ OUNCES BLENDED WHISKEY

SPARKLING WATER

LEMON PEEL TWIST, TO GARNISH

SERVES 1

SHAMROCK

1. Put cracked ice into a mixing glass.

2. Pour the whiskey, vermouth, and Chartreuse over the ice. Stir until well frosted.

3. Strain into a chilled cocktail glass, pour in the crème de menthe, and stir. Serve immediately.

INGREDIENTS

¾ OUNCE IRISH WHISKEY

¾ OUNCE DRY VERMOUTH

3 DASHES GREEN CHARTREUSE

3 DASHES CRÈME DE MENTHE

SERVES 1

MANHATTAN

1. Put cracked ice into a cocktail shaker.

2. Pour the liquid ingredients over the ice and shake vigorously until well frosted.

3. Strain into a chilled cocktail glass and garnish with the cherry. Serve immediately.

INGREDIENTS

DASH ANGOSTURA BITTERS

2½ OUNCES RYE WHISKEY

¾ OUNCE SWEET VERMOUTH

MARASCHINO CHERRY,
TO GARNISH

SERVES 1

OLD-FASHIONED

1. Put the sugar cube into a small, chilled old-fashioned glass.

2. Add the Angostura bitters and water. Stir until the sugar has dissolved.

3. Pour in the bourbon and stir.

4. Add the cracked ice and garnish with the lemon peel. Serve immediately.

INGREDIENTS

1 SUGAR CUBE

DASH ANGOSTURA BITTERS

1 TEASPOON WATER

1¾ OUNCES BOURBON OR
RYE WHISKEY

4-6 ICE CUBES, CRACKED

LEMON PEEL TWIST,
TO GARNISH

INGREDIENTS

4-6 ICE CUBES

1¾ OUNCES BOURBON

1 TEASPOON SUGAR SYRUP

CLUB SODA

½ OUNCE RUBY PORT

FRESHLY GRATED NUTMEG,
TO GARNISH

WHISKEY SANGAREE

1. Put the ice into a chilled glass.

2. Pour the bourbon and sugar syrup over the ice. Top with club soda.

3. Stir gently to mix, then float the port on top. Sprinkle with some of the grated nutmeg. Serve immediately.

BARTENDER'S TIP

Instead of bourbon whiskey, try a blended whiskey, or indeed any whiskey of your choice in this cocktail classic.

PINK HEATHER

1. Pour the whisky and the strawberry liqueur into a chilled champagne flute.

2. Top off with chilled sparkling wine and garnish with a strawberry. Serve immediately.

SERVES 1

INGREDIENTS

¾ OUNCE SCOTCH WHISKY

¾ OUNCE STRAWBERRY LIQUEUR

CHILLED SPARKLING WINE

FRESH STRAWBERRY, TO GARNISH

FLYING SCOTSMAN

1. Put some crushed ice into a blender.

2. Dash Angostura bitters over the ice, and add the whisky, vermouth, and sugar syrup.

3. Blend until slushy and pour into a small, chilled old-fashioned glass. Serve immediately.

INGREDIENTS

CRUSHED ICE

DASH ANGOSTURA BITTERS

1¼ OUNCES SCOTCH WHISKY

¾ OUNCE SWEET VERMOUTH

¼ TEASPOON SUGAR SYRUP

BEADLESTONE

1. Put some cracked ice into a mixing glass and pour the whisky and vermouth over the ice.

2. Stir well to mix and strain into a chilled cocktail glass. Serve immediately.

INGREDIENTS

CRACKED ICE

1¼ OUNCES SCOTCH WHISKY

1¼ OUNCES DRY VERMOUTH

SERVES 1

INGREDIENTS

CRACKED ICE

DASH ANGOSTURA BITTERS

1¾ OUNCES SCOTCH WHISKY

1¼ OUNCES SWEET VERMOUTH

THISTLE

1. Put some cracked ice into a mixing glass.

2. Dash Angostura bitters over the ice and pour in the whisky and vermouth.

3. Stir well to mix and strain into a chilled cocktail glass. Serve immediately.

SERVES 1

INGREDIENTS

1¾ OUNCES IRISH WHISKEY

¾ OUNCE IRISH MIST

¾ OUNCE TRIPLE SEC

1 TEASPOON LEMON JUICE

ICE

COLLEEN

1. Shake the liquid ingredients vigorously over ice until well frosted.

2. Strain into a chilled cocktail glass. Serve immediately.

SERVES 1

INGREDIENTS

½ OUNCE BRANDY

½ OUNCE FERNET BRANCA

½ OUNCE CRÈME DE MENTHE

THE REVIVER

1. Shake the liquids well over ice until frosted.

2. Strain into a wine glass and drink as quickly as possible.

BARTENDER'S TIP

This cocktail, as its name suggests, is supposed to revive after a night of heavy drinking.

MIDNIGHT COWBOY

1. Slowly blend together the brandy, coffee liqueur, cream, and ice in a blender until frothy.

2. Pour into a chilled cocktail glass. Top off with cola and serve immediately.

SERVES 1

INGREDIENTS

¾ OUNCE BRANDY

½ OUNCE COFFEE LIQUEUR

½ OUNCE CREAM, CHILLED

CRUSHED ICE

COLA

INGREDIENTS

1¾ OUNCES BRANDY

¾ OUNCE APRICOT BRANDY

¾ OUNCE LIME JUICE

1 TEASPOON WHITE RUM

ICE

CUBAN

1. Pour the liquid ingredients over ice and shake vigorously until well frosted.

2. Strain into a chilled cocktail glass and serve immediately.

INGREDIENTS

¾ OUNCE LEMON
OR LIME JUICE

2 OUNCES BRANDY

1 TEASPOON CONFECTIONERS'
SUGAR OR SUGAR SYRUP

ICE

LIME SLICE AND
MARASCHINO CHERRY,
TO GARNISH

BRANDY SOUR

1. Shake the lemon juice, brandy, and sugar well over ice and strain into a cocktail glass.

2. Garnish with a lime slice and a cherry and serve immediately.

SERVES 1

SIDECAR

1. Put cracked ice into a cocktail shaker. Pour the liquid ingredients over the ice.

2. Shake vigorously until well frosted.

3. Strain into a chilled cocktail glass and garnish with the orange peel. Serve immediately.

INGREDIENTS

1¾ OUNCES BRANDY

¾ OUNCE TRIPLE SEC

¾ OUNCE LEMON JUICE

ORANGE PEEL TWIST, TO GARNISH

SERVES 1

BRANDY JULEP

1. Fill a chilled old-fashioned glass with cracked ice.

2. Add the brandy, sugar syrup, and mint leaves, and stir well to mix.

3. Garnish with a sprig of fresh mint and a slice of lemon. Serve immediately.

INGREDIENTS

CRACKED ICE

1¾ OUNCES BRANDY

1 TEASPOON SUGAR SYRUP

4 FRESH MINT LEAVES

FRESH MINT SPRIG AND LEMON SLICE, TO GARNISH

SERVES 1

INGREDIENTS

1¾ OUNCES APRICOT BRANDY

¾ OUNCE DRY VERMOUTH

1¾ OUNCES ORANGE JUICE

DASH GRENADINE

ICE

PINK WHISKERS

1. Shake the liquid ingredients vigorously over ice until well frosted.

2. Strain the mixture into a chilled cocktail glass and serve immediately.

BARTENDER'S TIP

Float 1 ounce of port on top for an extra depth and flavor.

SERVES 1

INGREDIENTS

1¾ OUNCES BRANDY

¾ OUNCE VAN DER HUM

¾ OUNCE TIA MARIA

1 TEASPOON CREAM

ICE

GRATED CHOCOLATE,
TO GARNISH

FIRST NIGHT

1. Shake the liquid ingredients together over ice.

2. Strain into a chilled cocktail glass and garnish with some grated chocolate. Serve immediately.

HEAVENLY

SERVES 1

INGREDIENTS

1¼ OUNCES BRANDY

½ OUNCE CHERRY BRANDY

½ OUNCE PLUM BRANDY

**MARASCHINO CHERRIES,
TO GARNISH**

1. Put cracked ice into a mixing glass.

2. Pour the liquid ingredients over the ice and stir well to mix.

3. Strain into a chilled glass and garnish with maraschino cherries. Serve immediately.

SERVES 1

INGREDIENTS

¾ OUNCE CHERRY BRANDY

1¼ OUNCES PINEAPPLE JUICE

½ OUNCE KIRSCH

1 EGG WHITE

FROZEN MARASCHINO CHERRY,
TO GARNISH

CHERRY KITSCH

1. Shake the cherry brandy, pineapple juice, kirsch, and egg white well over crushed ice until frosted.

2. Pour into a chilled tall, thin glass and top with a frozen maraschino cherry. Serve immediately.

SERVES 1

GODDAUGHTER

1. Put some crushed ice into a blender and add the apple brandy, amaretto, and applesauce.

2. Blend until smooth, then pour the mixture, without straining, into a chilled glass.

3. Sprinkle with ground cinnamon and serve immediately.

INGREDIENTS

CRUSHED ICE

1¾ OUNCES APPLE BRANDY

¾ OUNCE AMARETTO

1 TEASPOON APPLESAUCE

**GROUND CINNAMON,
TO GARNISH**

SERVES 1

BEAGLE

1. Put cracked ice into a mixing glass.

2. Dash kümmel and lemon juice over the ice and pour in the brandy and cranberry juice.

3. Stir well to mix, strain into a chilled cocktail glass, and serve immediately.

INGREDIENTS

DASH KÜMMEL

DASH LEMON JUICE

1¾ OUNCES BRANDY

**¼ OUNCE
CRANBERRY JUICE**

SERVES 1

INGREDIENTS

¾ OUNCE BRANDY

¾ OUNCE DARK CRÈME
DE CACAO

¼ OUNCE HEAVY CREAM

**FRESHLY GRATED NUTMEG,
TO GARNISH**

BRANDY ALEXANDER

1. Put cracked ice into a cocktail shaker.

2. Pour the brandy, crème de cacao, and cream over the ice and shake vigorously until well frosted.

3. Strain into a chilled cocktail glass. Sprinkle with the grated nutmeg and serve immediately.

BARTENDER'S TIP

This is the perfect after-dinner cocktail to serve with a creamy, chocolate dessert.

HOT BRANDY CHOCOLATE

1. Heat the milk in a small saucepan until almost boiling.

2. Add the chocolate and sugar and stir over low heat until the chocolate has melted.

3. Pour into four warm heatproof glasses, then pour ¾ ounce of the brandy over the back of a spoon on top of each.

4. Top with the whipped cream and sprinkle with the grated nutmeg. Serve immediately.

SERVES 4

INGREDIENTS

4 CUPS MILK

4 OUNCES SEMISWEET CHOCOLATE, CHOPPED

2 TABLESPOONS SUGAR

3½ OUNCES BRANDY

½ CUP WHIPPED CREAM

FRESHLY GRATED NUTMEG OR UNSWEETENED COCOA POWDER, FOR SPRINKLING

BUBBLES

(BOTH NAUGHTY & NICE)

SERVES 1

INGREDIENTS

FEW DROPS CRÈME DE CASSIS,
OR TO TASTE

½ OUNCE BRANDY

CHILLED CHAMPAGNE

FRESH MINT SPRING,
TO GARNISH

KIR ROYALE

1. Put the cassis into the bottom of a champagne flute.

2. Add the brandy. Top off with champagne.

3. Garnish with the mint sprig and serve immediately.

SERVES 1

INGREDIENTS

¾ OUNCE CRÈME DE BANANE

¾ OUNCE RUM

FEW DROPS ANGOSTURA
BITTERS

SPARKLING WHITE WINE

DISCO DANCER

1. Shake the first three ingredients well over ice.

2. Pour into a chilled glass and top off with sparkling wine to taste. Serve immediately.

SERVES 1

DIAMOND FIZZ

1. Shake the gin, lemon juice, and sugar syrup over ice until well frosted.

2. Strain into a chilled flute. Top off with chilled champagne and serve immediately.

INGREDIENTS

1¾ OUNCES GIN

½ OUNCE LEMON JUICE

1 TEASPOON SUGAR SYRUP

CHILLED CHAMPAGNE

SERVES 1

CHAMPAGNE SIDECAR

1. Shake the bourbon, Cointreau, and lemon juice over ice and strain into a chilled flute.

2. Top off with chilled champagne and serve immediately.

INGREDIENTS

1¼ OUNCES BOURBON

¾ OUNCE COINTREAU

1½ TEASPOONS LEMON JUICE

CHILLED CHAMPAGNE

CHAMPAGNE COCKTAIL

SERVES 1

INGREDIENTS

1 SUGAR CUBE

2 DASHES ANGOSTURA BITTERS

¾ OUNCE BRANDY

CHILLED CHAMPAGNE

1. Put the sugar cube into the bottom of a chilled champagne flute.

2. Add the Angostura bitters and the brandy.

3. Top off with champagne and serve immediately.

CHAMPAGNE PICK-ME-UP

1. Put cracked ice into a cocktail shaker.

2. Pour the brandy, orange juice, lemon juice, and grenadine over the ice and shake vigorously until well frosted.

3. Strain into a chilled wine glass, top off with champagne, and serve immediately.

SERVES 1

INGREDIENTS

1¾ OUNCES BRANDY

¾ OUNCE ORANGE JUICE

¾ OUNCE LEMON JUICE

DASH GRENADINE

CHILLED CHAMPAGNE

SERVES 1

BUCK'S FIZZ

1. Fill a chilled flute halfway with orange juice, then gently pour in the chilled champagne. Serve immediately.

INGREDIENTS

1¾ OUNCES CHILLED FRESH ORANGE JUICE

1¾ OUNCES CHILLED CHAMPAGNE

SERVES 1

DUKE

1. Shake the triple sec, lemon juice, orange juice, egg white, and maraschino liqueur vigorously over cracked ice until well frosted.

2. Strain into a chilled wine glass and top off with chilled champagne. Serve immediately.

INGREDIENTS

¾ OUNCE TRIPLE SEC

½ OUNCE LEMON JUICE

½ OUNCE ORANGE JUICE

1 EGG WHITE

DASH MARASCHINO LIQUEUR

CHILLED CHAMPAGNE OR SPARKLING WINE

KISMET

1. Pour the gin and brandy into a chilled flute.

2. Trickle the ginger syrup slowly down the glass, then top off with champagne. Garnish with a slice of mango and serve immediately.

INGREDIENTS

¾ OUNCE GIN

¾ OUNCE APRICOT BRANDY

½ TEASPOON PRESERVED GINGER SYRUP

CHILLED CHAMPAGNE

FRESH MANGO SLICES, TO GARNISH

LONDON FRENCH 75

1. Shake the gin and lemon juice vigorously over cracked ice until well frosted.

2. Strain into a chilled glass and top off with champagne. Serve immediately.

INGREDIENTS

1¾ OUNCES LONDON GIN

¾ OUNCE LEMON JUICE

CHILLED CHAMPAGNE

SERVES 1

INGREDIENTS

1 LEMON WEDGE

SUPERFINE SUGAR

¾ OUNCE PEACH JUICE

2½ OUNCES CHILLED CHAMPAGNE

BELLINI

1. Rub the rim of a chilled champagne flute with the lemon wedge.

2. Put the sugar in a saucer, then dip the rim of the flute in it.

3. Pour the peach juice into the flute.

4. Top off with the champagne.

5. Serve immediately.

MIMOSA

1. Put cracked ice into a cocktail shaker.

2. Scoop out the passion fruit flesh into the shaker.

3. Add the curaçao and shake until frosted.

4. Strain into a chilled champagne flute, top off with champagne, and garnish with the star fruit slice.

5. Serve immediately.

SERVES 1

INGREDIENTS

1 PASSION FRUIT

½ OUNCE ORANGE CURAÇAO

CHILLED CHAMPAGNE

STAR FRUIT (CARAMBOLA) SLICE, TO GARNISH

SERVES 1

INGREDIENTS

½ OUNCE GRAPEFRUIT JUICE

1½ TEASPOONS TRIPLE SEC

1½ TEASPOONS MANDARINE LIQUEUR

ICE

CHILLED CHAMPAGNE

FROZEN CITRUS FRUIT SLICES,
TO GARNISH

SAN REMO

1. Mix the first three ingredients with ice in a tall glass.

2. Top off with champagne and garnish with slices of frozen fruit. Serve immediately.

SERVES 1

INGREDIENTS

¾ OUNCE GOLDEN RUM

½ OUNCE COINTREAU

CHILLED CHAMPAGNE

SPARKLING GOLD

1. Pour the rum and liqueur into a chilled champagne flute.

2. Top off with champagne. Serve immediately.

SERVES 1

THE BENTLEY

1. Mix the first three ingredients gently together in a chilled glass.

2. Add the ice cube and slowly pour in champagne to taste. Serve immediately.

INGREDIENTS

½ OUNCE COGNAC OR BRANDY

½ OUNCE PEACH LIQUEUR, PEACH BRANDY, OR SCHNAPPS

JUICE OF 1 PASSION FRUIT, STRAINED

1 ICE CUBE

CHILLED CHAMPAGNE

SERVES 24

RASPBERRY MIST

1. Blend the Irish Mist and raspberries in a blender with crushed ice.

2. When lightly frozen, strain between chilled champagne glasses and top off with wine.

3. Top each glass with a raspberry and serve immediately.

INGREDIENTS

5¼ OUNCES IRISH MIST

3½ CUPS RASPBERRIES

CRUSHED ICE

4 (750 ML) BOTTLES SPARKLING DRY WHITE WINE, WELL CHILLED

24 RASPBERRIES, TO GARNISH

WILD SILK

1. Set aside 2 unbruised raspberries. Blend the remainder with the cream, framboise, and some crushed ice in a blender until frosted and slushy.

2. Pour into chilled glasses and top off with champagne.

3. Float a raspberry on top and serve immediately.

SERVES 2

INGREDIENTS

A FEW RASPBERRIES

½ OUNCE CREAM

¾ OUNCE FRAMBOISE OR RASPBERRY SYRUP

CRUSHED ICE

CHILLED CHAMPAGNE

BLACK VELVET

1. Fill a glass halfway with stout, then slowly pour in an equal quantity of wine over the back of a spoon that is just touching the top of the stout and the edge of the glass. Serve immediately.

SERVES 1

INGREDIENTS

CHILLED STOUT

CHILLED SPARKLING WHITE WINE

BARTENDER'S TIP

Pouring the wine over the back of a spoon as described here should stop the drinks from mixing together and keep them in separate layers.

SERVES 1

ROYAL JULEP

1. In a small glass, crush the sugar and mint together with a little of the whiskey.

2. When the sugar has dissolved, strain it into a chilled glass with the rest of the whiskey, and top off with champagne.

3. Garnish with a mint sprig and serve immediately.

INGREDIENTS

1 SUGAR LUMP

3 SPRIGS FRESH MINT, PLUS EXTRA TO GARNISH

¾ OUNCE JACK DANIELS WHISKEY

CHILLED CHAMPAGNE

SERVES 1

CARIBBEAN CHAMPAGNE

1. Pour the rum and crème de banane into a chilled flute and top off with champagne.

2. Stir gently to mix and garnish with slices of banana. Serve immediately.

INGREDIENTS

½ OUNCE WHITE RUM

½ OUNCE CRÈME DE BANANE

CHILLED CHAMPAGNE

BANANA SLICES, TO GARNISH

SERVES 1

JADE

1. Shake the Midori, curaçao, lime juice, and Angostura bitters vigorously over cracked ice until well frosted.

2. Strain into a chilled flute. Top off with chilled champagne and garnish with a slice of lime. Serve immediately.

INGREDIENTS

1½ TEASPOONS MIDORI

1½ TEASPOONS BLUE CURAÇAO

1½ TEASPOONS LIME JUICE

DASH ANGOSTURA BITTERS

CHILLED CHAMPAGNE

LIME SLICE, TO GARNISH

SERVES 1

UNDER THE BOARDWALK

1. Blend crushed ice in a blender with the lemon juice, sugar syrup, and chopped peach until slushy.

2. Pour into a chilled glass, top off with sparkling water, and stir gently.

3. Garnish with raspberries and serve immediately.

INGREDIENTS

CRUSHED ICE

1¾ OUNCES LEMON JUICE

½ TEASPOON SUGAR SYRUP

½ PEACH, PEELED, PITTED, AND CHOPPED

SPARKLING WATER

RASPBERRIES, TO GARNISH

MONTE CARLO

1. Put ice cubes into a mixing glass, then pour the gin and lemon juice over the ice.

2. Stir until well chilled.

3. Strain into a chilled champagne flute and top off with champagne.

4. Drizzle the crème de menthe over the top and garnish with the mint sprig.

5. Serve immediately.

SERVES 1

INGREDIENTS

4-6 ICE CUBES

½ OUNCE GIN

1½ TEASPOONS LEMON JUICE

CHAMPAGNE OR SPARKLING WHITE WINE, CHILLED

¼ OUNCE CRÈME DE MENTHE

FRESH MINT SPRIG, TO GARNISH

FLIRTINI

SERVES 1

INGREDIENTS

¼ SLICE FRESH PINEAPPLE, CHOPPED

½ OUNCE CHILLED COINTREAU

½ OUNCE CHILLED VODKA

¾ OUNCE CHILLED
PINEAPPLE JUICE

CHILLED CHAMPAGNE

1. Put the pineapple into a mixing glass or bowl.

2. Crush the pineapple and add the Cointreau, vodka, and pineapple juice. Stir well.

3. Strain into a glass and top off with champagne.

4. Serve immediately.

PEACEMAKER

1. Put the fruit and sugar into a large punch bowl.

2. Add a little water and crush together.

3. Add the maraschino and sparkling water and mix well.

4. Top off with the champagne and garnish with the mint leaves and strawberry slices. Serve immediately.

INGREDIENTS

25 STRAWBERRIES, HULLED

½ SMALL FRESH PINEAPPLE, PEELED AND CRUSHED

1-2 TABLESPOONS CONFECTIONERS' SUGAR

¾ OUNCE MARASCHINO

1 CUP SPARKLING WATER

1 (750 ML) BOTTLE DRY CHAMPAGNE

FRESH MINT LEAVES AND SLICED STRAWBERRIES, TO GARNISH

SOUTHERN CHAMPAGNE

1. Pour the liqueur and bitters into a chilled champagne flute, and stir to mix.

2. Fill the glass with champagne. Drop the peel into the glass to garnish and serve immediately.

INGREDIENTS

¾ OUNCE SOUTHERN COMFORT

DASH ANGOSTURA BITTERS

CHILLED CHAMPAGNE

TWIST OF ORANGE PEEL, TO GARNISH

AMARETTINE

SERVES 1

1. Mix the amaretto and vermouth in a chilled tall cocktail glass. Top off with wine to taste and serve immediately.

INGREDIENTS

2 TEASPOONS AMARETTO

2 TEASPOONS DRY VERMOUTH

SPARKLING WHITE WINE

SABRINA

SERVES 1

1. Shake the first five ingredients together over ice.

2. Pour into a tall champagne flute and top off with sparkling wine.

3. Garnish with slices of orange and lemon and serve immediately.

INGREDIENTS

½ OUNCE GIN

¾ TEASPOON APRICOT BRANDY

½ OUNCE FRESH ORANGE JUICE

1 TEASPOON GRENADINE

1½ TEASPOONS CINZANO

ICE

SWEET SPARKLING WINE

ORANGE AND LEMON SLICES,
TO GARNISH

SERVES 2

INGREDIENTS

12 OUNCES (1½ CUPS) COLD
SPARKLING WHITE WINE

1¾ OUNCES CRÈME DE CASSIS

¾ OUNCE BRANDY

CRUSHED ICE

**BLACKBERRIES,
TO GARNISH**

PINK SHERBET ROYALE

1. Blend half the wine in a blender with the cassis, brandy, and ice until really cold and frosted.

2. Slowly whisk in a little more wine and pour into tall glasses.

3. Garnish with the blackberries and serve immediately.

KIR LETHALE

1. Put the raisin into the bottom of a chilled champagne flute.

2. Pour in the crème de cassis and vodka.

3. Fill the glass with sparkling wine and serve immediately.

SERVES 1

INGREDIENTS

1 RAISIN SOAKED IN VODKA

½ OUNCE CRÈME DE CASSIS

1 TEASPOON VODKA

SPARKLING WINE

INGREDIENTS

¾ OUNCE SWEET VERMOUTH

¾ OUNCE CAMPARI BITTERS

SPARKLING WINE

HALF A THIN ORANGE SLICE,
TO GARNISH

BROKEN NEGRONI

1. Add the vermouth and bitters to a mixing glass filled with ice, and stir.

2. Strain into a chilled champagne flute.

3. Top off with sparkling wine, then garnish the glass with the orange slice. Serve immediately.

INGREDIENTS

½ OUNCE BOURBON

1½ TEASPOONS TRIPLE SEC

2 DASHES ANGOSTURA BITTERS

2 DASHES PEYCHAUD'S
AROMATIC BITTERS

SPARKLING WINE

ORANGE TWIST, TO GARNISH

SEELBACH

1. Pour the bourbon and triple sec into a chilled champagne flute.

2. Add the bitters.

3. Top with sparkling wine.

4. Garnish the glass with the orange twist and serve immediately.

SERVES 1

DEATH IN THE AFTERNOON

INGREDIENTS

¾ OUNCE PASTIS

SPARKLING WINE

LEMON TWIST,
TO GARNISH

1. Pour the pastis into a chilled champagne flute.

2. Top off with sparkling wine.

3. Garnish the glass with the lemon twist and serve immediately.

SERVES 1

THE QUEEN'S COUSIN

INGREDIENTS

¾ OUNCE VODKA

½ OUNCE ORANGE-FLAVORED LIQUEUR

½ OUNCE FRESH LIME JUICE

1 TEASPOON TRIPLE SEC

DASH ANGOSTURA BITTERS

SPARKLING WINE

1. Pour the vodka, orange-flavored liqueur, fresh lime juice, triple sec, and bitters into a shaker filled with cracked ice.

2. Shake well and strain into a chilled wine glass.

3. Fill the glass with sparkling wine and serve immediately.

MIDNIGHT'S KISS

1. Spread the sugar on a plate. Run a wedge of lemon around the rim of a chilled champagne flute to moisten it, then dip the glass in the sugar.

2. Add the vodka and curaçao to a shaker filled with cracked ice.

3. Shake well, strain into the glass, and top off with sparkling wine. Serve immediately.

SERVES 1

INGREDIENTS

SUGAR

LEMON WEDGE

½ OUNCE VODKA

2 TEASPOONS BLUE CURAÇAO

SPARKLING WINE

BARTENDER'S TIP

You can use any sugar around the rim of the glass—or buy gold sugar from a speciality supplier to increase the glamour factor of this cocktail.

SERVES 1

INGREDIENTS

¾ OUNCE LEMON-LIME SODA

¾ OUNCE CRANBERRY JUICE

ICE

SPARKLING WINE

**MINT SPRIG,
TO GARNISH**

PRETTY
IN PINK

1. Pour the soda and juice into an old-fashioned glass filled with ice cubes.

2. Stir gently.

3. Fill the glass with the wine.

4. Garnish with the mint sprig and serve immediately.

SERVES 4

INGREDIENTS

1 TABLESPOON RAISINS
OR CHOPPED PRUNES

1 OUNCE BRANDY

10 OUNCES (1¼ CUPS)
SPARKLING WHITE WINE OR
CHAMPAGNE, CHILLED

10 OUNCES (1¼ CUPS) WHITE
CRANBERRY AND GRAPE JUICE

ICE CUBES

SAN JOAQUIN PUNCH

1. Mix the dried fruit and brandy in a small bowl and let soak for 1-2 hours.

2. In a pitcher, mix the sparkling wine, juice, and soaked fruit.

3. Pour into ice-filled glasses and serve immediately.

SERVES 1

INGREDIENTS

GRENADINE

SUGAR

½ OUNCE PEAR LIQUEUR

½ OUNCE TRIPLE SEC

1¼ OUNCES GRAPEFRUIT JUICE

SPARKLING WINE

ROYAL SILVER

1. Dip the rim of a wine glass first into some grenadine and then into some sugar.

2. Pour the pear liqueur, triple sec, and juice into a shaker filled with cracked ice.

3. Shake well and strain carefully into the chilled glass.

4. Top off with sparkling wine and serve immediately.

SERVES 1

MARILYN MONROE

1. Add the brandy and grenadine to a chilled champagne glass and stir.

2. Top off with sparkling wine.

3. Hang the cherries over the edge of the glass to garnish and serve immediately.

INGREDIENTS

¾ OUNCE APPLE BRANDY

1 TEASPOON GRENADINE

SPARKLING WINE

2 MARASCHINO CHERRIES, TO GARNISH

SERVES 1

NIGHT & DAY

1. Pour the sparkling wine into a chilled champagne flute.

2. Slowly add the brandy and the orange-flavored liqueur, then add the bitters. Serve immediately.

INGREDIENTS

2½ OUNCES SPARKLING WINE

½ OUNCE BRANDY

2 TEASPOONS ORANGE-FLAVORED LIQUEUR

1 TEASPOON CAMPARI BITTERS

THE STONE FENCE

1. Add the bourbon and bitters to a chilled highball glass filled with ice.

2. Top off with the cider.

3. Garnish with the mint sprig and serve immediately.

SERVES 1

INGREDIENTS

1¼ OUNCES BOURBON

2 DASHES ANGOSTURA BITTERS

ICE

SPARKLING HARD CIDER

SPRIG OF MINT, BRUISED, TO GARNISH

SERVES 1

INGREDIENTS

4 OUNCES SPARKLING HARD
CIDER OR APPLE JUICE

¾ OUNCE APPLE BRANDY

JUICE OF ½ LEMON

1 TABLESPOON EGG WHITE

GENEROUS PINCH SUGAR

ICE

SLICES OF LEMON AND APPLE,
TO GARNISH

APPLE FIZZ

1. Shake the first five ingredients together over ice.

2. Pour immediately into a glass.

3. Garnish with a slice of lemon and apple and serve immediately.

SERVES 1

INGREDIENTS

¾ OUNCE COCONUT RUM

ICE

SPARKLING HARD CIDER

APPLE SLICE, TO GARNISH

APPLE BREEZE

1. Add the liqueur to a chilled highball glass filled halfway with ice.

2. Top off with the cider.

3. Garnish the glass with the apple slice and serve immediately.

SERVES 4

INGREDIENTS

2 LEMONS

1 CUP CONFECTIONERS' SUGAR

1 CUP RASPBERRIES

FEW DROPS VANILLA EXTRACT

CRACKED ICE

SPARKLING WATER

FRESH MINT SPRIGS, TO GARNISH

RASPBERRY LEMONADE

1. Cut the ends off the lemons, then scoop out and chop the flesh.

2. Put the lemon flesh into a blender with the sugar, raspberries, vanilla extract, and cracked ice and blend for 2-3 minutes.

3. Fill four highball glasses halfway with cracked ice and strain in the blended mixture.

4. Top off with sparkling water and garnish with the mint sprigs. Serve immediately.

SERVES 1

BLOOD ON THE TRACKS

1. Pour the bitters into a chilled highball glass filled with ice.

2. Add the juice. Do not stir.

3. Top off with sparkling water.

4. Garnish with the orange slice and mint and serve immediately.

INGREDIENTS

½ OUNCE CAMPARI BITTERS

ICE

2 OUNCES BLOOD ORANGE JUICE

SPARKLING WATER

ORANGE SLICE AND MINT SPRIG, TO GARNISH

SERVES 1

COOL COLLINS

1. Put the mint leaves into a chilled tall glass.

2. Add the sugar and lemon juice.

3. Crush the mint leaves, then stir until the sugar has dissolved.

4. Fill the glass with cracked ice and top off with sparkling water.

5. Stir gently and garnish with the fresh mint and lemon slice. Serve immediately.

INGREDIENTS

6 FRESH MINT LEAVES, PLUS EXTRA TO GARNISH

1 TEASPOON SUPERFINE SUGAR

1¾ OUNCES LEMON JUICE

CRACKED ICE

SPARKLING WATER

LEMON SLICE, TO GARNISH

SERVES 1

INGREDIENTS

CRACKED ICE

1¾ OUNCES HAZELNUT SYRUP

1¾ OUNCES LEMON JUICE

1 TEASPOON GRENADINE

SPARKLING WATER

HEAVENLY DAYS

1. Put cracked ice into a cocktail shaker.

2. Pour the hazelnut syrup, lemon juice, and grenadine over the ice. Shake vigorously until well frosted.

3. Fill a glass halfway with cracked ice and strain the cocktail over it.

4. Top off with sparkling water and stir gently.

5. Serve immediately.

BARTENDER'S TIP

This is the perfect alcohol-free cocktail to indulge in on a hot summer's day.

SUMMER PUNCH

1. Pour the wine into a punch bowl or large glass serving bowl. Add the honey and stir well. Add the brandy, if using.

2. Cut any large berries into bite-size pieces and put all the berries and mint sprigs into the wine.

3. Let stand for 15 minutes, then add the sparkling water and ice cubes. Ladle the punch into glasses or punch cups making sure each has an ice cube and a few pieces of fruit. Serve immediately, garnished with mint sprigs.

SERVES 8

INGREDIENTS

1 (750 ML) ROSÉ WINE, CHILLED

1 TABLESPOON HONEY

5 OUNCES BRANDY (OPTIONAL)

1 CUP MIXED BERRIES, SUCH AS RASPBERRIES, BLUEBERRIES, AND HULLED STRAWBERRIES

3-4 FRESH MINT SPRIGS, PLUS EXTRA TO GARNISH

2½ CUPS SPARKLING WATER, CHILLED

ICE CUBES

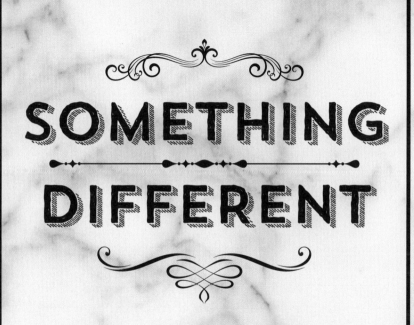

SOMETHING
DIFFERENT

SERVES 1

EL DIABLO

1. Add the tequila, juice, and cassis to a shaker filled with ice. Shake well.

2. Strain into a chilled highball glass filled with ice.

3. Top off with ginger ale. Garnish the glass with the lime. Serve immediately.

INGREDIENTS

¾ OUNCE TEQUILA

½ OUNCE FRESH LIME JUICE

½ OUNCE CRÈME DE CASSIS

CRACKED ICE

GINGER ALE

LIME SLICE, TO GARNISH

SERVES 1

EL TORO

1. Pour the tequila, coffee liqueur, and cream into a shaker filled with cracked ice.

2. Shake well and strain into a chilled cocktail glass. Serve immediately.

INGREDIENTS

1¾ OUNCES TEQUILA

¾ OUNCE COFFEE LIQUEUR

¾ OUNCE LIGHT CREAM

SERVES 1

HIGH VOLTAGE

1. Pour the tequila, schnapps, and juice into a shaker filled with cracked ice.

2. Shake well and strain into a chilled cocktail glass.

3. Garnish the glass with the peach slice and serve immediately.

INGREDIENTS

1¾ OUNCES TEQUILA

¾ OUNCE PEACH SCHNAPPS

½ OUNCE FRESH LIME JUICE

FRESH PEACH SLICE, PEELED, TO GARNISH

SERVES 1

SILK STOCKINGS

1. Pour the tequila, liqueurs, and cream into a shaker filled with cracked ice.

2. Shake well and strain into a chilled cocktail glass.

3. Garnish the glass with raspberries on a toothpick. Serve immediately.

INGREDIENTS

1¼ OUNCES TEQUILA

½ OUNCE RASPBERRY LIQUEUR

½ OUNCE CRÈME DE CACAO

¾ OUNCE HEAVY CREAM

FRESH RASPBERRIES, TO GARNISH

TEQUILA SLAMMER

1. Put the tequila into a chilled glass.

2. Add the lemon juice.

3. Top off with sparkling wine.

4. Cover the glass with your hand and slam to mix.

5. Serve immediately.

SERVES 1

INGREDIENTS

¾ OUNCE SILVER TEQUILA, CHILLED

JUICE OF ½ LEMON

CHILLED SPARKLING WINE

TEQUILA SUNRISE

1. Put the cracked ice into a chilled highball glass. Pour the tequila over the ice.

2. Top off with orange juice.

3. Stir well to mix.

4. Slowly pour the grenadine over the juice. Garnish with the orange slice and maraschino cherry.

5. Serve immediately.

SERVES 1

INGREDIENTS

4–6 ICE CUBES, CRACKED

1¼ OUNCES SILVER TEQUILA

ORANGE JUICE

¾ OUNCE GRENADINE

ORANGE SLICE AND
MARASCHINO CHERRY,
TO GARNISH

INGREDIENTS

1¾ OUNCES VODKA

¾ OUNCE COFFEE LIQUEUR

CRACKED ICE

BLACK RUSSIAN

1. Pour the vodka and liqueur over cracked ice in a chilled old-fashioned glass.

2. Stir to mix and serve immediately.

INGREDIENTS

1 TEASPOON CRÈME DE MENTHE

½–1 OUNCE HEAVY CREAM

1¾ OUNCES COFFEE LIQUEUR OR CHOCOLATE LIQUEUR

CHOCOLATE MATCHSTICKS, TO SERVE

JEALOUSY

1. Gently beat the crème de menthe into the cream until thick.

2. Pour the coffee liqueur into a chilled shot glass, then carefully spoon the flavored whipped cream over the liqueur.

3. Serve immediately with the chocolate matchsticks.

BANANA SLIP

1. Pour the chilled crème de banane into a chilled shot glass.

2. With a steady hand, gently pour in the chilled cream liqueur to make a second layer. Serve immediately.

SERVES 1

INGREDIENTS

¾ OUNCE CRÈME DE BANANE, CHILLED

¾ OUNCE IRISH CREAM LIQUEUR, CHILLED

BLOODY BRAIN

1. Pour the peach schnapps into a shot glass, then carefully pour the cream liqueur on top.

2. Finally, pour in the grenadine and serve immediately.

SERVES 1

INGREDIENTS

¾ OUNCE PEACH SCHNAPPS, CHILLED

1 TEASPOON IRISH CREAM LIQUEUR, CHILLED

½ TEASPOON GRENADINE, CHILLED

SERVES 1

INGREDIENTS

¾ OUNCE BRANDY

¾ OUNCE DRY VERMOUTH

¾ OUNCE DUBONNET

BVD

1. Pour the brandy, dry vermouth, and Dubonnet over cracked ice in a mixing glass.

2. Stir to mix and strain into a chilled wine glass. Serve immediately.

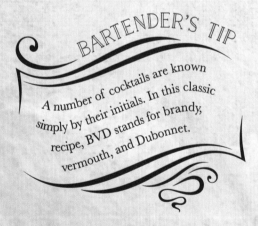

BARTENDER'S TIP

A number of cocktails are known simply by their initials. In this classic recipe, BVD stands for brandy, vermouth, and Dubonnet.

INGREDIENTS

1¾ OUNCES SLOE GIN

ORANGE JUICE

CRACKED ICE

ORANGE SLICE, TO GARNISH

SLOE SCREW

1 Shake the sloe gin and orange juice over cracked ice until well frosted and pour into a chilled glass.

2 Garnish with the orange slice and serve immediately.

AFRICAN MINT

SERVES 1

INGREDIENTS

¾ OUNCE CRÈME DE MENTHE, CHILLED

¾ OUNCE AMARULA, CHILLED

1. Pour the crème de menthe into a chilled shot glass, reserving a few drops.

2. Pour the Amarula slowly over the back of a spoon to create a second layer.

3. Drizzle the remaining drops of crème de menthe over the creamy liqueur to finish. Serve immediately.

ZANDER

SERVES 1

INGREDIENTS

CRACKED ICE

¾ OUNCE SAMBUCA

¾ OUNCE ORANGE JUICE

DASH LEMON JUICE

BITTER LEMON

1. Fill a chilled glass with cracked ice.

2. Shake the Sambuca, orange juice, and lemon juice vigorously over cracked ice until well frosted.

3. Strain into the glass and top off with bitter lemon. Serve immediately.

FRENCH KISS

1. Put cracked ice into a cocktail shaker.

2. Pour the liquid ingredients over the ice and shake vigorously until well frosted.

3. Strain into a chilled cocktail glass and serve immediately.

SERVES 1

INGREDIENTS

1¾ OUNCES BOURBON

¾ OUNCE APRICOT LIQUEUR

2 TEASPOONS GRENADINE

1 TEASPOON LEMON JUICE

QUEEN OF MEMPHIS

1. Put cracked ice into a cocktail shaker.

2. Pour the bourbon, Midori, peach juice, and maraschino over the ice and shake vigorously until well frosted.

3. Strain into a chilled cocktail glass. Garnish with the melon wedge and serve immediately.

SERVES 1

INGREDIENTS

1¾ OUNCES BOURBON

¾ OUNCE MIDORI

¾ OUNCE PEACH JUICE

DASH MARASCHINO LIQUEUR

MELON WEDGE, TO GARNISH

RATTLESNAKE

1. Pour the chilled crème de cacao into a shot glass.

2. With a steady hand, gently pour in the chilled cream liqueur over the back of a spoon to make a second layer.

3. Pour in the chilled Kahlúa to make a third layer. Do not stir. Serve immediately.

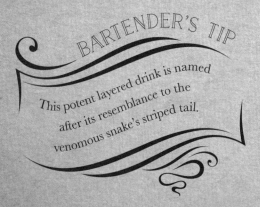

SERVES 1

INGREDIENTS

¾ OUNCE DARK CRÈME DE CACAO, CHILLED

¾ OUNCE IRISH CREAM LIQUEUR, CHILLED

¾ OUNCE KAHLÚA, CHILLED

BARTENDER'S TIP

This potent layered drink is named after its resemblance to the venomous snake's striped tail.

AFTER FIVE

SERVES 1

INGREDIENTS

½ OUNCE PEPPERMINT SCHNAPPS, CHILLED

¾ OUNCE KAHLÚA, CHILLED

½ OUNCE IRISH CREAM LIQUEUR

1. Pour the peppermint schnapps into a chilled small wine glass.

2. Carefully pour the Kahlúa over the back of a spoon to make a second layer.

3. Finally, float the cream liqueur on top. Serve immediately.

SERVES 1

INGREDIENTS

1 TEASPOON GREEN CRÈME
DE MENTHE

½ OUNCE ICED WATER

¾ OUNCE WHITE CRÈME
DE MENTHE

1¾ OUNCES APPLE OR PEAR SCHNAPPS

SERVES 2

INGREDIENTS

1¾ OUNCES GOLDEN RUM

¾ OUNCE GALLIANO

1¾ OUNCES PINEAPPLE JUICE

1½ TEASPOONS LIME JUICE

¾ OUNCE SUGAR SYRUP

PINEAPPLE SHELL, TO SERVE

CHAMPAGNE

LIME AND LEMON SLICES
AND CHERRIES, TO GARNISH

MINTED DIAMONDS

1. Mix the green crème de menthe with the water. Pour into an ice cube tray and freeze.

2. Stir the white crème de menthe and apple or pear schnapps over ice until well frosted.

3. Strain the cocktail into a chilled cocktail glass and add the mint ice cubes. Drink when the ice cubes begin to melt.

JOSIAH'S BAY FLOAT

1. Put cracked ice into a cocktail shaker.

2. Pour the rum, Galliano, pineapple juice, lime juice, and sugar syrup over the ice and shake vigorously until well frosted.

3. Strain into the pineapple shell.

4. Top off with champagne and garnish with the lime and lemon slices and maraschino cherries. Serve immediately.

MELLOW MULE

SERVES 2

1. Put cracked ice into a cocktail shaker.

2. Pour the white rum, dark rum, golden rum, falernum, and lime juice over the ice and shake vigorously until well frosted.

3. Strain the cocktail into tall, chilled glasses.

4. Top off with ginger beer and garnish with pineapple wedges and ginger. Serve immediately.

INGREDIENTS

1¾ OUNCES WHITE RUM

¾ OUNCE DARK RUM

¾ OUNCE GOLDEN RUM

**¼ OUNCE FALERNUM
(WINE GINGER SYRUP)**

¾ OUNCE LIME JUICE

GINGER BEER

PINEAPPLE WEDGES
AND GINGER, TO GARNISH

BANANA DAIQUIRI

SERVES 1

1. Put all the liquid ingredients into a blender.

2. Add the banana and blend until smooth.

3. Pour, without straining, into a chilled glass.

4. Garnish with the lime slice and serve immediately.

INGREDIENTS

1¾ OUNCES WHITE RUM, CHILLED

½ OUNCE TRIPLE SEC, CHILLED

½ OUNCE LIME JUICE

½ OUNCE LIGHT CREAM, CHILLED

1 TEASPOON SUGAR SYRUP

¼ BANANA, PEELED AND SLICED

LIME SLICE, TO GARNISH

CAIPIRINHA

SERVES 1

INGREDIENTS

6 LIME WEDGES

2 TEASPOONS GRANULATED SUGAR

2½ OUNCES CACHAÇA

CRACKED ICE

1. Put the lime wedges in a chilled old-fashioned glass.

2. Add the sugar.

3. Muddle the lime wedges, then pour the cachaça over the citrus.

4. Fill the glass with the cracked ice and stir well.

5. Serve immediately.

SERVES 1

INGREDIENTS

1¾ OUNCES BOURBON

2½ OUNCES MILK

DASH VANILLA EXTRACT

1 TEASPOON HONEY

FRESHLY GRATED NUTMEG,
TO GARNISH

BOURBON MILK PUNCH

1. Put cracked ice into a cocktail shaker.

2. Pour the bourbon, milk, and vanilla extract over the ice.

3. Add the honey and shake until well frosted.

4. Strain into a chilled glass. Sprinkle with the grated nutmeg.

5. Serve immediately.

CHERRY COLA

1. Fill a chilled old-fashioned glass halfway with cracked ice.

2. Pour the cherry brandy and lemon juice over the ice.

3. Top off with cola, stir gently, and garnish with a slice of lemon. Serve immediately.

SERVES 1

INGREDIENTS

CRACKED ICE

1¼ OUNCES CHERRY BRANDY

¾ OUNCE LEMON JUICE

COLA

LEMON SLICE

BLUE LAGOON

1. Pour the curaçao into a chilled martini glass, followed by the vodka.

2. Add the lemon juice and top off with the soda. Serve immediately.

SERVES 1

INGREDIENTS

¾ OUNCE BLUE CURAÇAO

¾ OUNCE VODKA

DASH LEMON JUICE

LEMON-LIME SODA

SERVES 1

TORNADO

1. Pour the schnapps into a chilled shot glass.

2. Gently pour in the sambuca over the back of a spoon.

3. Let stand for a few minutes to settle and separate before drinking.

INGREDIENTS

¾ OUNCE PEACH OR OTHER SCHNAPPS, FROZEN

¾ OUNCE BLACK SAMBUCA, FROZEN

SERVES 1

WHITE DIAMOND FRAPPÉ

1. Shake the peppermint schnapps, white crème de cacao, anise liqueur, and lemon juice over some crushed ice until frosted.

2. Strain into a chilled old-fashioned glass and add a small spoonful of crushed ice. Serve immediately.

INGREDIENTS

1½ TEASPOONS PEPPERMINT SCHNAPPS

1½ TEASPOONS WHITE CRÈME DE CACAO

1½ TEASPOONS ANISE LIQUEUR

1½ TEASPOONS LEMON JUICE

CRUSHED ICE

B-52

1. Pour the crème de cacao into a shot glass.

2. With a steady hand, gently pour in the cream liqueur to make a second layer.

3. Gently pour in the Grand Marnier.

4. Cover with your hand and slam to mix, or alternatively serve with layers intact.

5. Serve immediately.

SERVES 1

INGREDIENTS

¾ OUNCE CHILLED DARK
CRÈME DE CACAO

¾ OUNCE CHILLED IRISH CREAM
LIQUEUR

¾ OUNCE CHILLED
GRAND MARNIER

SERVES 1

INGREDIENTS

¾ OUNCE CHILLED RED
MARASCHINO LIQUEUR

¾ OUNCE CHILLED
CRÈME DE MENTHE

¾ OUNCE CHILLED
IRISH CREAM LIQUEUR

FRESH MINT LEAF, TO GARNISH

1. Pour the maraschino into a chilled shot glass.

2. Gently pour in the crème de menthe to make a second layer.

3. Gently pour in the cream liqueur.

4. Garnish with the mint leaf.

5. Serve immediately.

SERVES 1

SHADY LADY

1. Shake the tequila, apple brandy, cranberry juice, and a dash of lime juice over ice cubes until well frosted.

2. Strain into a chilled cocktail glass and serve immediately.

INGREDIENTS

2½ OUNCES TEQUILA

¾ OUNCE APPLE BRANDY

¾ OUNCE CRANBERRY JUICE

DASH LIME JUICE

SERVES 1

MOO MOO

1. Pour the liqueurs and cream into a cocktail shaker filled with cracked ice.

2. Shake well and strain into a chilled highball glass filled with ice cubes.

3. Sprinkle a little cinnamon on top and serve immediately.

INGREDIENTS

¾ OUNCE IRISH CREAM LIQUEUR

¾ OUNCE CRÈME DE CACAO

2½ OUNCES LIGHT CREAM

ICE CUBES

GROUND CINNAMON, TO GARNISH

SERVES 1

CLIMAX

1. Pour the liqueurs and cream into a cocktail shaker filled with cracked ice.

2. Shake well and strain into a chilled old-fashioned glass filled with ice cubes. Serve immediately.

INGREDIENTS

¾ OUNCE IRISH CREAM LIQUEUR

¾ OUNCE ALMOND-FLAVORED LIQUEUR

¾ OUNCE COFFEE LIQUEUR

¾ OUNCE LIGHT CREAM

ICE CUBES

SERVES 1

PEACH FLOYD

1. Stir all the liquid ingredients together over cracked ice.

2. Pour into a chilled small glass and serve immediately.

INGREDIENTS

¾ OUNCE PEACH SCHNAPPS, CHILLED

¾ OUNCE VODKA, CHILLED

¾ OUNCE WHITE CRANBERRY AND PEACH JUICE, CHILLED

¾ OUNCE CRANBERRY JUICE, CHILLED

CRACKED ICE

SERVES 6

INGREDIENTS

JUICE OF 1 ORANGE

JUICE OF 1 LEMON

2 TABLESPOONS
CONFECTIONERS' SUGAR

CRACKED ICE

1 ORANGE, THINLY SLICED

1 LEMON, THINLY SLICED

1 BOTTLE CHILLED RED WINE

LEMON-LIME SODA, TO TASTE

SANGRIA

1. Put the orange juice and lemon juice in a large pitcher. Stir.

2. Add the sugar and stir. When the sugar has dissolved, add cracked ice, sliced fruit, and wine and marinate for 1 hour.

3. Add lemon-lime soda to taste, then top off with cracked ice. Serve immediately.

BARTENDER'S TIP

You can vary the combination of fruit according to taste and availability.

INGREDIENTS

1¾ OUNCES DARK CRÈME
DE CACAO

¾ OUNCE CRÈME DE NOYAUX

¾ OUNCE LIGHT CREAM

PINK
SQUIRREL

1. Pour the crème de cacao, crème de noyaux, and light cream over cracked ice and shake vigorously until well frosted.

2. Strain into a chilled cocktail glass and serve immediately.

FIRELIGHTER

SERVES 1

INGREDIENTS

¾ OUNCE ABSINTHE, ICED

¾ OUNCE LIME SYRUP, ICED

1. Shake the absinthe and lime syrup vigorously over cracked ice until well frosted.

2. Strain into a chilled shot glass and serve immediately.

AMARETTO COFFEE

SERVES 1

INGREDIENTS

1¼ OUNCES AMARETTO

SUGAR

FRESHLY MADE STRONG BLACK COFFEE

½–1 OUNCE HEAVY CREAM

1. Put the amaretto into a warm heatproof glass and add sugar to taste.

2. Pour in the coffee and stir.

3. When the sugar has completely dissolved, pour in the cream slowly over the back of a spoon so that it floats on top.

4. Don't stir—drink the coffee through the cream.

SERVES 1

INGREDIENTS

1¾ OUNCES AMARETTO

¾ OUNCE WHITE CRÈME DE MENTHE

AMARETTO STINGER

1. Shake the amaretto and white crème de menthe vigorously over cracked ice until well frosted.

2. Strain into a chilled old-fashioned glass and serve immediately.

SERVES 1

INGREDIENTS

1¼ OUNCES KAHLÚA

1¼ OUNCES IRISH CREAM LIQUEUR

1¼ OUNCES VODKA

MUDSLIDE

1. Shake the Kahlúa, cream liqueur, and vodka vigorously over cracked ice until well frosted.

2. Strain into a chilled glass and serve immediately.

SERVES 1

INGREDIENTS

¾ OUNCE IRISH CREAM
LIQUEUR

**¾ OUNCE WHITE CRÈME
DE MENTHE**

IRISH STINGER

1. Shake the cream liqueur and white crème de menthe vigorously over cracked ice until well frosted.

2. Strain into a chilled shot or old-fashioned glass.

BARTENDER'S TIP

Substitute the Irish cream liqueur for 1¾ ounces of brandy to make the classic Stinger cocktail instead.

WHITE COSMOPOLITAN

1. Shake the limoncello, Cointreau, and white cranberry and grape juice over cracked ice until frosted.

2. Strain into a chilled glass.

3. Add the bitters, garnish with the cranberries, and serve immediately.

SERVES 1

INGREDIENTS

1¼ OUNCES LIMONCELLO

½ OUNCE COINTREAU

¾ OUNCE WHITE CRANBERRY AND GRAPE JUICE

DASH ORANGE BITTERS

CRANBERRIES, TO GARNISH

CHOCOLATE MARTINI

1. Moisten the rim of a cocktail glass with an orange slice. Dip in the cocoa powder and set aside.

2. Shake the vodka, crème de cacao, and orange flower water over ice cubes until really well frosted.

3. Strain into the cocktail glass and garnish with a twist of orange peel. Serve immediately.

INGREDIENTS

ORANGE SLICE

UNSWEETENED COCOA POWDER

1¾ OUNCES VODKA

¼ OUNCE CRÈME DE CACAO

2 DASHES ORANGE FLOWER WATER

ORANGE PEEL TWIST

ALABAMA SLAMMER

1. Pour the Southern Comfort, amaretto, and sloe gin over cracked ice in a mixing glass and stir.

2. Strain into a shot glass and add the lemon juice. Cover with your hand, slam on the table, and drink immediately.

INGREDIENTS

¾ OUNCE SOUTHERN COMFORT

¾ OUNCE AMARETTO

¾ OUNCE SLOE GIN

½ TEASPOON LEMON JUICE

TOFFEE SPLIT

SERVES 1

1. Fill a shot glass with crushed ice.

2. Pour the Drambuie over the ice, then pour in the toffee liqueur over the back of a spoon to make a layer on top. Serve immediately.

INGREDIENTS

CRUSHED ICE

1¾ OUNCES DRAMBUIE

¾ OUNCE TOFFEE LIQUEUR, ICED

VOODOO

SERVES 1

1. Pour the Kahlúa, Malibu, butterscotch schnapps, and milk into a chilled shot glass.

2. Stir well. Serve immediately.

INGREDIENTS

½ OUNCE KAHLÚA

½ OUNCE MALIBU, CHILLED

½ OUNCE BUTTERSCOTCH SCHNAPPS, CHILLED

¾ OUNCE MILK, CHILLED

SERVES 1

INGREDIENTS

1 OUNCE COGNAC

¾ OUNCE DARK CRÈME DE CACAO

¼ OUNCE CRÈME DE BANANE

½ OUNCE CREAM

NAPOLEON'S NIGHTCAP

1. Stir the cognac, crème de cacao, and crème de banane in a mixing glass with cracked ice.

2. Strain into a chilled cocktail glass and float the cream on top. Serve immediately.

BARTENDER'S TIP

Instead of hot chocolate at bedtime, Napoleon apparently knocked back a chocolate-laced brandy with a hint of banana.

IRISH COFFEE

1. Put the whiskey into a warm heatproof glass and add sugar to taste.

2. Pour in the coffee and stir.

3. When the sugar has completely dissolved, pour in the cream slowly over the back of a spoon so that it floats on top.

4. Don't stir—drink the coffee through the cream.

SERVES 1

INGREDIENTS

1¾ OUNCES IRISH WHISKEY

SUGAR

FRESHLY MADE STRONG
BLACK COFFEE

1¾ OUNCES HEAVY CREAM

MOCKTAILS

INGREDIENTS

5¼ OUNCES MILK
2½ OUNCES CREAM OF COCONUT
3½ OUNCES PINEAPPLE JUICE
CRACKED ICE CUBES

TO GARNISH

PINEAPPLE CHUNK
PINEAPPLE LEAF
MARASCHINO CHERRY

MINI COLADA

1. Put cracked ice into a cocktail shaker.

2. Pour the milk and cream of coconut over the ice.

3. Add the pineapple juice and shake vigorously until well frosted.

4. Fill a highball glass halfway with cracked ice, strain the cocktail into it, and garnish with the pineapple chunk, pineapple leaf, and cherry. Serve immediately.

INGREDIENTS

1¾ OUNCES LEMON JUICE
½ OUNCE GRENADINE
½ OUNCE SUGAR SYRUP
CRACKED ICE
GINGER ALE
ORANGE SLICE, TO GARNISH

SHIRLEY TEMPLE

1. Put cracked ice into a cocktail shaker.

2. Pour the lemon juice, grenadine, and sugar syrup over the ice and shake vigorously until well frosted.

3. Fill a chilled highball glass halfway with cracked ice, then strain the cocktail over it.

4. Top off with ginger ale and garnish with the orange slice. Serve immediately.

INGREDIENTS

2½ OUNCES PINEAPPLE JUICE

1¾ OUNCES LIME JUICE

¾ OUNCE GREEN PEPPERMINT SYRUP

CRACKED ICE

GINGER ALE

CUCUMBER STRIP AND LIME SLICE, TO GARNISH

BRIGHT GREEN COOLER

1. Put cracked ice into a cocktail shaker.

2. Pour the two juices and peppermint syrup over the ice. Shake vigorously until well frosted.

3. Fill a chilled highball glass halfway with cracked ice and strain the cocktail over it.

4. Top off with ginger ale and garnish with the cucumber strip and lime slice. Serve immediately.

INGREDIENTS

6 OUNCES ORANGE JUICE

6 OUNCES SPARKLING WHITE GRAPE JUICE

ORANGE SLICES, TO GARNISH

MAIDENLY MIMOSA

1. Chill two champagne flutes.

2. Divide the orange juice between the flutes and top off with the sparkling grape juice.

3. Garnish with the orange slices and serve immediately.

SERVES 6

INGREDIENTS

1½ CUPS APPLE JUICE
1¹/₂ CUPS LEMON JUICE
½ CUP SUGAR SYRUP
CRACKED ICE
2 LITERS GINGER ALE
ORANGE SLICES,
TO GARNISH

PROHIBITION PUNCH

1. Pour the apple juice into a large pitcher.

2. Add the lemon juice and sugar syrup and a handful of cracked ice.

3. Add the ginger ale and stir gently to mix. Pour into chilled old-fashioned glasses and garnish with the orange slices. Serve immediately.

BARTENDER'S TIP

This is the perfect punch to serve to children at a summer party.

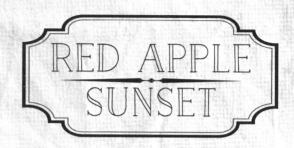

RED APPLE SUNSET

SERVES 1

INGREDIENTS

1¾ OUNCES APPLE JUICE
1¾ OUNCES GRAPEFRUIT JUICE
DASH GRENADINE

1. Shake the apple juice, grapefruit juice, and a dash of grenadine over ice cubes until well frosted.

2. Strain into a chilled cocktail glass and serve immediately.

FAUX KIR ROYALE

1. Put cracked ice into a mixing glass. Pour the raspberry syrup over the ice.

2. Stir well to mix and strain into a chilled wine glass.

3. Top off with sparkling apple juice and stir. Serve immediately.

SERVES 1

INGREDIENTS

1¼ OUNCES
RASPBERRY SYRUP

CHILLED SPARKLING APPLE
JUICE

RANCH GIRL

1. Shake the lime juice, barbecue sauce, and dashes of Worcestershire sauce and hot pepper sauce over ice cubes until well frosted.

2. Pour into a chilled highball glass, top off with tomato juice, and stir.

3. Garnish with a couple of slices of lime and a pickled jalapeño chile. Serve immediately.

SERVES 1

INGREDIENTS

¾ OUNCE LIME JUICE

¾ OUNCE BARBECUE SAUCE

WORCESTERSHIRE SAUCE

HOT PEPPER SAUCE

ICE CUBES

TOMATO JUICE

LIME SLICES AND
1 PICKLED JALAPEÑO CHILE,
TO GARNISH

BABY BELLINI

1 Pour the peach juice and lemon juice into a chilled champagne flute and stir well.

2 Top off with sparkling apple juice and stir again. Serve immediately.

SERVES 1

INGREDIENTS

1¾ OUNCES PEACH JUICE

¾ OUNCE LEMON JUICE

SPARKLING APPLE JUICE

BITE OF THE APPLE

1 Blend some crushed ice in a blender with the apple juice, lime juice, orgeat syrup, and applesauce until smooth.

2 Pour into a chilled old-fashioned glass and sprinkle with cinnamon. Serve immediately.

SERVES 1

INGREDIENTS

CRUSHED ICE

4¼ OUNCES APPLE JUICE

¾ OUNCE LIME JUICE

½ TEASPOON ORGEAT SYRUP

½ OUNCE APPLESAUCE

GROUND CINNAMON

SERVES 1

INGREDIENTS

2½ OUNCES TOMATO JUICE

¾ OUNCE LEMON JUICE

2 DASHES WORCESTERSHIRE
SAUCE

1 DASH HOT PEPPER SAUCE

PINCH CELERY SALT

PEPPER

LEMON WEDGE AND
CELERY STALK, TO GARNISH

VIRGIN MARY

1. Put cracked ice into a cocktail
shaker. Pour the tomato juice over
the ice.

2. Add the lemon juice.

3. Pour in the Worcestershire
sauce and hot pepper sauce. Shake
vigorously until well frosted.

4. Season to taste with the celery
salt and pepper, strain into a
chilled glass, and garnish with
the lemon wedge and celery stalk.

5. Serve immediately.

SERVES 6

INGREDIENTS

16 OUNCES (2 CUPS)
TOMATO JUICE

3 OUNCES (1 CUP) ORANGE JUICE

2½ OUNCES LIME JUICE

½ OUNCE HOT PEPPER SAUCE

**2 TEASPOONS
WORCESTERSHIRE SAUCE**

1 JALAPEÑO CHILE, SEEDED
AND FINELY CHOPPED

CELERY SALT

WHITE PEPPER (PREFERABLY
FRESHLY GROUND)

CRACKED ICE

SANGRÍA SECA

1. Pour the three juices and the hot pepper and Worcestershire sauces into a pitcher.

2. Add the chile and season with the celery salt and white pepper.

3. Stir well and chill in the refrigerator for at least an hour.

4. To serve, fill chilled highball glasses halfway with cracked ice and strain the cocktail over it.

5. Serve immediately.

KNICKS VICTORY COOLER

SERVES 1

1. Fill a chilled highball glass halfway with the cracked ice.

2. Pour the apricot juice over the ice, top off with raspberry juice, and stir gently.

3. Garnish with an orange peel twist and fresh raspberries. Serve immediately.

INGREDIENTS

CRACKED ICE

1¼ OUNCES APRICOT JUICE

RASPBERRY JUICE

ORANGE PEEL TWIST AND A
FEW RASPBERRIES, TO GARNISH

SERVES 2

NEW ENGLAND PARTY

1. Put all the ingredients, except the seasoning and celery stalk, into a blender and blend until smooth.

2. Transfer to a pitcher, cover, and chill in the refrigerator for about an hour.

3. Pour into two chilled highball glasses and season to taste.

4. Garnish with a celery stalk and serve immediately.

INGREDIENTS

CRUSHED ICE

DASH HOT PEPPER SAUCE

DASH WORCESTERSHIRE SAUCE

1 TEASPOON LEMON JUICE

1 CARROT, CHOPPED

2 CELERY STALKS, CHOPPED

10 OUNCES (1¼ CUPS) TOMATO JUICE

5 OUNCES CLAM JUICE

SALT AND FRESHLY GROUND
BLACK PEPPER

CELERY STALKS, TO GARNISH

SERVES 2

FRUIT COOLER

1. Pour the orange juice and yogurt into a food processor and process gently until combined.

2. Add the eggs and frozen bananas and process until smooth.

3. Pour the mixture into highball or hurricane glasses and garnish the rims with slices of fresh banana. Serve immediately.

INGREDIENTS

3 OUNCES (1 CUP) ORANGE JUICE

½ CUP PLAIN YOGURT

2 EGGS

2 BANANAS, SLICED AND FROZEN

FRESH BANANA SLICES

SERVES 1

CITRUS FIZZ

1. Rub the rim of a champagne flute with orange or lime juice and dip into the confectioners' sugar.

2. Stir the rest of the juices together with the bitters and then pour into the glass.

3. Add sparkling water to taste and serve immediately.

INGREDIENTS

1¼ OUNCES FRESH ORANGE JUICE, CHILLED

CONFECTIONERS' SUGAR

SQUEEZE LIME JUICE

FEW DROPS ANGOSTURA BITTERS

1¼-2½ OUNCES SPARKLING WATER, CHILLED

MANGO LASSI

SERVES 2

INGREDIENTS

8 OUNCES (1 CUP) MILK

½ CUP PLAIN YOGURT

½ OUNCE ROSE WATER

3 TABLESPOONS HONEY

1 RIPE MANGO, PEELED
AND DICED

4–6 ICE CUBES

ROSE PETALS, TO GARNISH
(OPTIONAL)

1. Pour the milk and yogurt into a blender and process until combined.

2. Add the rose water and honey and process until blended.

3. Add the mango and ice cubes and blend until smooth.

4. Pour into two chilled glasses and garnish with the rose petals, if using.

5. Serve immediately.

COCONUT CREAM

1. Pour the pineapple juice and coconut milk into a blender.

2. Add the ice cream and process until smooth.

3. Add the pineapple chunks and process until smooth.

4. Divide between two chilled glasses and garnish with the grated coconut.

5. Serve immediately.

SERVES 2

INGREDIENTS

12 OUNCES (1½ CUPS) PINEAPPLE JUICE

3 OUNCES COCONUT MILK

1 CUP VANILLA ICE CREAM

1 CUP FROZEN PINEAPPLE CHUNKS

GRATED FRESH COCONUT, TO GARNISH

COCOBERRY

1. Rub the raspberries through a strainer with the back of a spoon and transfer the puree to a blender.

2. Add the crushed ice, cream of coconut, and pineapple juice and blend until smooth, then pour the mixture, without straining, into a chilled old-fashioned glass.

3. Garnish with a pineapple wedge and fresh raspberries. Serve immediately.

SERVES 1

INGREDIENTS

¾ CUP RASPBERRIES

CRUSHED ICE

¾ OUNCE CREAM OF COCONUT

5 OUNCES PINEAPPLE JUICE

PINEAPPLE WEDGE

A FEW RASPBERRIES

COCOBELLE

1. Blend the first four ingredients in a blender until slushy.

2. Chill a tall glass and gently dribble a few splashes of grenadine down the insides.

3. Pour in the slush slowly and top with the toasted coconut. Serve immediately.

SERVES 1

INGREDIENTS

2½ OUNCES COLD MILK

¾ OUNCE CREAM OF COCONUT

2 SCOOPS VANILLA ICE CREAM

3–4 ICE CUBES

DASH GRENADINE

DRIED COCONUT, TOASTED, TO GARNISH

SLUSH PUPPY

1. Pour the lemon juice and grenadine into a chilled tall glass with ice.

2. Add the lemon peel, syrup, and club soda to taste. Garnish with a cherry and serve immediately.

INGREDIENTS

JUICE OF 1 LEMON
OR ½ PINK GRAPEFRUIT

1 OUNCE GRENADINE

ICE CUBES

FEW LEMON PEEL STRIPS

½ OUNCE RASPBERRY SYRUP

CLUB SODA

MARASCHINO CHERRY, TO GARNISH

THAI FRUIT COCKTAIL

1. Shake the ingredients over crushed ice in a cocktail shaker.

2. Pour into a chilled tall glass and finish with a flower. Serve immediately.

INGREDIENTS

2 OUNCES PINEAPPLE JUICE

2 OUNCES ORANGE JUICE

½ OUNCE LIME JUICE

2 OUNCES PASSION FRUIT JUICE

3½ OUNCES GUAVA JUICE

CRUSHED ICE

FLOWER, TO GARNISH

SERVES 1

INGREDIENTS

4-6 ICE CUBES, CRACKED

3½ OUNCES APPLE JUICE

1 SMALL SCOOP, VANILLA
ICE CREAM

CLUB SODA

**CINNAMON SUGAR AND
APPLE, TO GARNISH**

APPLE PIE CREAM

1. Put the cracked ice into a blender and add the apple juice and ice cream.

2. Blend for 10-15 seconds, until frothy and frosted. Pour into a glass and top off with club soda.

3. Sprinkle with the cinnamon sugar and garnish with an apple slice. Serve immediately.

BARTENDER'S TIP

For an alcoholic version of this sweet treat, use hard apple cider instead of the apple juice.

PEACHY CREAM

1. Pour the peach juice and cream together over ice cubes and shake vigorously until well frosted.

2. Fill a chilled highball glass or old-fashioned glass halfway with cracked ice and strain the cocktail over it. Serve immediately.

SERVES 1

INGREDIENTS

1¾ OUNCES PEACH JUICE, CHILLED

1¾ OUNCES LIGHT CREAM

CRACKED ICE

SERVES 1

INGREDIENTS

GINGER ALE

FRESH MINT SPRIGS, PLUS EXTRA TO GARNISH

CRACKED ICE

FRESH RASPBERRIES, TO GARNISH

GINGER FIZZ

1. Put 1¾ ounces of ginger ale into a blender, add a few mint sprigs, and blend together.

2. Strain into a chilled highball glass filled two-thirds of the way with cracked ice and top off with more ginger ale.

3. Garnish with raspberries and the mint sprig. Serve immediately.

SERVES 1

INGREDIENTS

2 OUNCES GRENADINE

2 OUNCES FRESH LEMON OR LIME JUICE

ICE CUBES

LEMON-LIME SODA

FRESH LEMON OR LIME SLICES, TO GARNISH

SOBER SUNDAY

1. Pour the grenadine and fruit juice into a highball glass filled with ice cubes.

2. Top off with the soda and finish with slices of lemon and lime. Serve immediately.

SERVES 1

LONG BOAT

1. Fill a chilled glass two-thirds of the way with ice cubes and pour in the lime syrup.

2. Top off with ginger beer and stir gently.

3. Garnish with the lime wedge and the mint sprig. Serve immediately.

INGREDIENTS

ICE CUBES

¾ OUNCE LIME SYRUP

GINGER BEER

LIME WEDGE AND MINT SPRIG, TO GARNISH

SERVES 2

CRANBERRY ENERGIZER

1. Pour the cranberry juice and orange juice into a blender and blend gently until combined.

2. Add the raspberries and lemon juice and blend until smooth.

3. Strain into glasses and garnish with the slices of orange. Serve immediately.

INGREDIENTS

10 OUNCES (1¼ CUPS) CRANBERRY JUICE

4 OUNCES ORANGE JUICE

½ CUP FRESH RASPBERRIES

½ OUNCE LEMON JUICE

FRESH ORANGE SLICES, TO GARNISH

THE GUNNER

1. Mix all the ingredients together in a long glass.

2. Taste and add more Angostura bitters if you wish. Serve immediately.

SERVES 1

INGREDIENTS

4-6 ICE CUBES

2 OUNCES LIME JUICE

2-3 DASHES ANGOSTURA BITTERS, OR TO TASTE

7 OUNCES GINGER BEER

7 OUNCES LEMON-LIME SODA

BARTENDER'S TIP

The Gunner is renowned for being light and refreshing, perfect for a hot summer evening.

PEAR & RASPBERRY DELIGHT

1. Put the pears into a blender with the raspberries and water and blend until smooth.

2. Taste and sweeten with honey if the raspberries are a little sharp.

3. Strain into glasses and garnish with the raspberries. Serve immediately.

SERVES 2

INGREDIENTS

2 LARGE RIPE ANJOU PEARS, PEELED, CORED, AND CHOPPED

1 CUP FROZEN RASPBERRIES

6 OUNCES ICE-COLD WATER

HONEY, TO TASTE

RASPBERRIES, TO GARNISH

SERVES 2

INGREDIENTS

1 POUND STRAWBERRIES

4 OUNCES CREAM OF COCONUT

2½ CUPS CHILLED PINEAPPLE
JUICE

STRAWBERRY COLADA

1. Reserve four strawberries to garnish. Hull and halve the remainder and place in the blender.

2. Add the cream of coconut and pineapple juice and blend until smooth, then pour into chilled glasses and garnish with the reserved strawberries. Serve immediately.

SERVES 1

INGREDIENTS

ICE CUBES

1¾ OUNCES ORANGE JUICE

1¾ OUNCES BITTER LEMON

ORANGE AND LEMON SLICES,
TO GARNISH

ST. CLEMENTS

1. Put some ice cubes into a chilled glass. Pour in the orange juice and bitter lemon.

2. Stir gently and garnish with the slices of orange and lemon. Serve immediately.

SERVES 2

INGREDIENTS

10 OUNCES (1¼ CUPS) MILK

¼ CUP INSTANT COFFEE POWDER

1 CUP VANILLA ICE CREAM

2 BANANAS, SLICED AND
FROZEN, PLUS EXTRA SLICES
TO GARNISH

BROWN SUGAR, TO TASTE

BANANA COFFEE BREAK

1. Pour the milk into a food processor, add the coffee powder, and process gently until combined. Add half the vanilla ice cream and process gently, then add the remaining ice cream and process until well combined.

2. When thoroughly blended, add the bananas and sugar to taste and process until smooth.

3. Pour into chilled glasses and serve, garnished with a few slices of banana. Serve immediately.

SERVES 1

INGREDIENTS

3½ OUNCES PINEAPPLE JUICE

1¾ OUNCES CREAM OF COCONUT

CUP OF CRUSHED ICE

PINEAPPLE CHUNK AND
MARASCHINO CHERRY,
TO GARNISH

COCO COLADA

1. Pour the juice and cream of coconut into a blender and add the ice.

2. Blend until combined and slushy and pour into a chilled glass.

3. Garnish the glass with the pineapple and maraschino cherry on a toothpick. Serve immediately.

SERVES 10

INGREDIENTS

6 CUPS GRAPE JUICE

10 OUNCES (1¼ CUPS)
ORANGE JUICE

2½ OUNCES CRANBERRY
JUICE

2 OUNCES LEMON JUICE

2 OUNCES LIME JUICE

3½ OUNCES SUGAR SYRUP

ICE CUBES

LEMON, ORANGE, AND LIME
SLICES, TO GARNISH

SOFT SANGRIA

1. Put the grape juice, orange juice, cranberry juice, lemon juice, lime juice, and sugar syrup into a chilled punch bowl and stir well.

2. Add ice cubes and garnish with the slices of lemon, orange, and lime.

SERVES 1

INGREDIENTS

CRACKED ICE

1¾ OUNCES ORANGE JUICE

¾ OUNCE LEMON JUICE

¾ OUNCE GRENADINE

SPARKLING MINERAL WATER

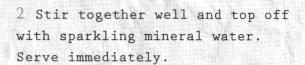

SUNRISE

1. Put cracked ice into a chilled highball glass and pour the orange juice, lemon juice, and grenadine over it.

2. Stir together well and top off with sparkling mineral water. Serve immediately.

INGREDIENTS

JUICE OF ½ LEMON

1 EGG WHITE

1 DASH GRENADINE

CRUSHED ICE

LEMON-LIME SODA

LEMON SLICE,
TO GARNISH

POM POM

1. Shake the lemon juice, egg white, and grenadine together and strain over crushed ice in a tall glass.

2. Top off with lemon-lime soda and garnish with a lemon slice on the rim of the glass. Serve immediately.

INGREDIENTS

CRACKED ICE

2 BANANAS

8 OUNCES (1 CUP) PINEAPPLE JUICE,
CHILLED

4 OUNCES LIME JUICE

**PINEAPPLE SLICES,
TO GARNISH**

PERKY PINEAPPLE

1. Put cracked ice into a blender. Peel the bananas and slice directly into the blender. Add the pineapple and lime juice and blend until smooth.

2. Pour into chilled glasses and garnish with the slices of pineapple. Serve immediately.

MOCHA SLUSH

SERVES 1

1. Blend crushed ice in a small blender with the coffee and chocolate syrups and milk until slushy.

2. Pour into a chilled glass and sprinkle with grated chocolate. Serve immediately.

INGREDIENTS

CRUSHED ICE

3½ OUNCES COFFEE SYRUP

1½ OUNCES CHOCOLATE SYRUP

7 OUNCES MILK

GRATED CHOCOLATE

MOCHA CREAM

SERVES 2

1. Put the milk, cream, and sugar into a food processor or blender and process gently until combined.

2. Add the cocoa powder and coffee syrup and process well, then add the ice cubes and process until smooth.

3. Pour the mixture into glasses. Top with whipped cream, sprinkle with the grated chocolate, and serve immediately.

INGREDIENTS

7 OUNCES MILK

2 OUNCES LIGHT CREAM

1 TABLESPOON BROWN SUGAR

2 TABLESPOONS UNSWEETENED COCOA POWDER

½ OUNCE COFFEE SYRUP OR INSTANT COFFEE POWDER

6 ICE CUBES

WHIPPED CREAM AND GRATED CHOCOLATE, TO GARNISH

INGREDIENTS

ICE CUBES

2½ OUNCES LEMON-LIME SODA

2½ OUNCES ICED TEA

ARNOLD PALMER

1. Fill a chilled highball glass halfway with ice cubes and pour in the soda.

2. Slowly pour in the tea, so that it does not mix.

3. Serve immediately with a straw.

BARTENDER'S TIP

This refreshing combination of iced tea and lemon-lime soda is named after American golfer Arnold Palmer.

SALTY PUPPY

SERVES 1

INGREDIENTS

GRANULATED SUGAR
KOSHER SALT
LIME WEDGE
CRACKED ICE
½ OUNCE LIME JUICE
GRAPEFRUIT JUICE

1. Mix equal quantities of the sugar and salt together on a saucer.

2. Rub the rim of a chilled highball glass with a wedge of lime and dip it into the sugar and salt mixture to frost.

3. Fill the glass with cracked ice and pour the lime juice over it. Top off with grapefruit juice and serve immediately.

CLAM DIGGER

SERVES 1

INGREDIENTS

HOT PEPPER SAUCE

WORCESTERSHIRE SAUCE

3½ OUNCES TOMATO JUICE

3½ OUNCES CLAM JUICE

¼ TEASPOON HORSERADISH SAUCE

CRACKED ICE

CELERY SALT AND PEPPER

CELERY STALK AND LIME WEDGE, TO GARNISH

1. Put 4-6 ice cubes into a cocktail shaker. Dash the hot pepper and Worcestershire sauce over the ice, pour in the tomato juice and clam juice, and add the horseradish sauce. Shake vigorously until frosted.

2. Fill a chilled highball glass with cracked ice and strain the cocktail over it. Season to taste with celery salt and pepper and garnish with a celery stalk and lime wedge. Serve immediately.

COCONUT ISLANDER

SERVES 4

INGREDIENTS

1 PINEAPPLE

3½ OUNCES PINEAPPLE JUICE

1 OUNCE CREAM OF COCONUT

4 OUNCES MILK

2 TABLESPOONS CRUSHED PINEAPPLE

3 TABLESPOONS COCONUT FLAKES

CRUSHED ICE

CHERRIES AND PINEAPPLE LEAVES, TO GARNISH

1. Cut the top off the pineapple and remove the flesh. Use some of the flesh and set aside the rest for a salad or dessert.

2. Blend all the liquid ingredients in a blender with the coconut flakes and some crushed ice for 30-40 seconds.

3. When smooth and frothy, pour into the pineapple shell, garnish with cherries or the pineapple leaves, and serve immediately with straws.

CRANBERRY PUNCH

1. Put the first six ingredients into a saucepan and bring to a boil. Reduce the heat to low and simmer for 5 minutes.

2. Remove from the heat and pour into a heatproof pitcher or bowl. Chill in the refrigerator.

3. Remove from the refrigerator, put cracked ice into the serving glasses, pour in the punch, and garnish with cranberries on toothpicks.

SERVES 10

INGREDIENTS

2½ CUPS CRANBERRY JUICE

2½ CUPS ORANGE JUICE

5 OUNCES WATER

½ TEASPOON GROUND GINGER

¼ TEASPOON CINNAMON

¼ TEASPOON GRATED NUTMEG

CRACKED ICE

CRANBERRIES, TO GARNISH

NONALCOHOLIC PIMM'S

1. Mix the first six ingredients together thoroughly in a large pitcher or punch bowl.

2. Float in the fruit and mint, keep in a cold place, and add the ice cubes just before serving.

SERVES 6

INGREDIENTS

2½ CUPS LEMON-LIME SODA, CHILLED

2 CUPS COLA, CHILLED

2 CUPS DRY GINGER ALE, CHILLED

JUICE OF 1 ORANGE

JUICE OF 1 LEMON

FEW DROPS ANGOSTURA BITTERS

SLICED FRUIT AND MINT SPRIGS, TO GARNISH

ICE CUBES

A Sloe Kiss 21
absinthe: Firelighter 148
African Mint 132
After Five 135
Alabama Slammer 152
Alaska 26
amaretto
  A Sloe Kiss 21
  Alabama Slammer 152
  Amarettine 107
  Amaretto Coffee 148
  Amaretto Stinger 149
  Goddaughter 85
  Ocean Breeze 61
Amarula
  African Mint 132
  Vodka Espresso 53
Apple Breeze 118
Apple Fizz 117
Apple Pie Cream 172
Arnold Palmer 184
Aurora Borealis 46

B-52 142
Baby Bellini 163
Bachelor's Bait 35
Bajan Sun 60
Banana Coffee Break 179
Banana Colada 56
Banana Daiquiri 137
Banana Slip 129
Beadlestone 76
Beagle 85
Belle Collins 19
Bellini 96
Bite of the Apple 163
Black Beauty 42
Black Russian 128
Black Velvet 101
Bleu Bleu Bleu 31
Blood On The Tracks 119
Bloodhound 25
Bloody Brain 129
Bloody Caesar 44
Bloody Mary 44
Blue Blooded 30
Blue Hawaiian 61
Blue Lagoon 140
Blue Monday 43
Boston Sour 71
Bourbon Milk Punch 139
brandy
  Bajan Sun 60
  Beagle 85
  Brandy Alexander 86
  Brandy Julep 81
  Brandy Sour 80
  BVD 130
  Champagne Cocktail 92
  Champagne
    Pick-Me-Up 93
  Cherry Cola 140
  Cherry Kitsch 84
  Cuban 80
  First Night 83
  Goddaughter 85
  Heavenly 84
  Hot Brandy Chocolate 87
  Kir Royale 90
  Kismet 95
  Marilyn Monroe 115
  Midnight Cowboy 79
  Napoleon's Nightcap 154
  Night & Day 115
  Peartini 41
  Pink Sherbet Royale 108
  Pink Whiskers 82
  Sabrina 107
  San Joaquin Punch 114
  Shady Lady 144
  Sidecar 81
  Singapore Sling 18
  Summer Punch 121

The Bentley 99
The Reviver 78
Wedding Belle 27
Bride's Mother 27
Bright Green Cooler 159
Broken Negroni 110
Buck's Fizz 94
BVD 130

Caipirinha 138
Caribbean Champagne 102
champagne
  Bellini 96
  Buck's Fizz 94
  Caribbean
    Champagne 102
  Champagne Cocktail 92
  Champagne
    Pick-Me-Up 93
  Champagne Sidecar 91
  Diamond Fizz 91
  Duke 94
  Flirtini 105
  Jade 103
  Josiah's Bay Float 136
  Kir Royale 90
  Kismet 95
  London French 75 95
  Mimosa 97
  Monte Carlo 104
  Peacemaker 106
  Royal Julep 102
  San Joaquin Punch 114
  San Remo 98
  Southern Champagne 106
  Sparkling Gold 98
  The Bentley 99
  Wild Silk 100
Chartreuse
  Alaska 26
  Aurora Borealis 46
  Green Lady 34
  Shamrock 72
Cherry Cola 140
Cherry Kitsch 84
Chocolate Martini 152
cider, hard
  Apple Breeze 118
  Apple Fizz 117
  The Stone Fence 116
Citrus Fizz 167
Clam Digger 186
Climax 145
Club Mojito 59
Coco Colada 179
Cocobelle 170
Cocoberry 170
Coconut Cream 169
Coconut Islander 186
coffee liqueur
  Black Russian 128
  Climax 145
  El Toro 124
  First Night 83
  Jealousy 128
  Midnight Cowboy 79
Cointreau
  Blue Monday 43
  Champagne Sidecar 91
  Flirtini 105
  Sparkling Gold 98
  White Cosmopolitan 151
Colleen 77
Cool Collins 119
Cordless Screwdriver 43
Cosmopolitan 36
Cranberry Collins 50
Cranberry Energizer 175
Cranberry Punch 187
crème de banane
  Banana Slip 129
  Caribbean
    Champagne 102

Disco Dancer 90
Napoleon's Nightcap 154
crème de cacao
  B-52 142
  Brandy Alexander 86
  Chocolate Martini 152
  Flying Grasshopper 46
  Moo Moo 144
  Napoleon's Nightcap 154
  Pink Squirrel 147
  Rattlesnake 134
  Silk Stockings 125
  White Diamond
    Frappé 141
crème de cassis
  Aurora Borealis 46
  El Diablo 124
  Kir Lethale 109
  Kir Royale 90
crème de menthe
  African Mint 132
  Amaretto Stinger 149
  Flying Grasshopper 46
  Irish Stinger 150
  Jealousy 128
  Long Island Iced Tea 45
  Minted Diamonds 136
  Monte Carlo 104
  Shamrock 72
  The Reviver 78
  Tricolor 143
Creole Lady 35
Cuba Libre 64
Cuban 80
Cuban Special 64
curaçao
  Aurora Borealis 46
  Bleu Bleu Bleu 31
  Blue Blooded 30
  Blue Hawaiian 61
  Blue Lagoon 140
  Blue Monday 43
  Firefly 22
  Jade 103
  Mai Tai 62
  Midnight's Kiss 112
  Mimosa 97
  Ocean Breeze 61
  The Blue Train 33

Daiquiri 56
Daisy 24
Death In The Afternoon 111
Diamond Fizz 91
Disco Dancer 90
Drambuie, Toffee Split 153
Dubonnet
  BVD 130
  Wedding Belle 27
Duke 94

El Diablo 124
El Toro 124

Faux Kir Royale 162
Firefly 22
Firelighter 148
First Night 83
Flirtini 105
Flying Grasshopper 46
Flying Scotsman 76
French Kiss 133
Frozen Peach Daiquiri 66
Fruit Cooler 167
Fuzzy Navel 38

Galliano
  A Sloe Kiss 21
  Harvey Wallbanger 40
  Josiah's Bay Float 136
gin
  A Sloe Kiss 21
  Alabama Slammer 152

Alaska 26
Bachelor's Bait 35
Belle Collins 19
Bleu Bleu Bleu 31
Bloodhound 25
Blue Blooded 30
Bride's Mother 27
Creole Lady 35
Daisy 24
Diamond Fizz 91
Firefly 22
Gin Rickey 20
Gin Sling 23
Grand Royal Clover
  Club 32
Green Lady 34
Hawaiian Orange
  Blossom 26
Kismet 95
London French 75 95
Long Island Iced Tea 45
Maiden's Prayer 23
Martini 18
Monte Carlo 104
Moonlight 28
Palm Beach 22
Pussycat 31
Sabrina 107
Saketini 34
Sloe Screw 131
Seventh Heaven 29
Singapore Sling 18
Teardrop 30
The Blue Train 33
Tom Collins 19
Wedding Belle 27
Ginger Fizz 174
Goddaughter 85
Grand Royal Clover Club 32
Green Lady 34

Harvey Wallbanger 40
Hawaiian Orange
  Blossom 26
Heavenly 84
Heavenly Days 120
High Voltage 125
Highland Fling 69
Hot Brandy Chocolate 87
Hurricane 57

Irish Coffee 155
Irish cream liqueur
  After Five 135
  B-52 142
  Banana Slip 129
  Bloody Brain 129
  Climax 145
  Irish Stinger 150
  Moo Moo 144
  Mudslide 149
  Rattlesnake 134
  Tricolor 143
Irish Mist
  Colleen 77
  Raspberry Mist 99

Jade 103
Jealousy 128
Josiah's Bay Float 136

Kahlúa
  After Five 135
  Mudslide 149
  Rattlesnake 134
  Voodoo 153
Kamikaze 39
Kir Lethale 109
Kir Royale 90
kirsch
  Cherry Kitsch 84
  Moonlight 28
Kismet 95

Klondike Cooler 72
Knicks Victory Cooler 166

Last Mango in Paris 47
London French 75 95
Long Boat 175
Long Island Iced Tea 45

Mai Tai 62
Maidenly Mimosa 159
Maiden's Prayer 23
Malibu
   Banana Colada 56
   Voodoo 153
Mango Lassi 168
Manhattan 73
maraschino
   Duke 94
   Peacemaker 106
   Queen of Memphis 133
   Seventh Heaven 29
   Tricolor 143
Marilyn Monroe 115
Martini 18
Mellow Mule 137
Metropolitan 52
Miami Beach 70
Midnight Cowboy 79
Midnight's Kiss 112
Midori
   Jade 103
   Queen of Memphis 133
Mimi 48
Mimosa 97
Mini Colada 158
Minted Diamonds 136
Mocha Cream 183
Mocha Slush 183
Monte Carlo 104
Moo Moo 144
Moonlight 28
Moscow Mule 51
Mudslide 149

Napoleon's Nightcap 154
New England Party 166
Night & Day 115
Nonalcoholic Pimm's 187

Ocean Breeze 61
Old-Fashioned 73

Palm Beach 22
Peacemaker 106
Peach Floyd 145
Peachy Cream 173
Pear & Raspberry
   Delight 177
Peartini 41
Perky Pineapple 182
Piña Colada 58
Pink Heather 75
Pink Sherbet Royale 108
Pink Squirrel 147
Pink Whiskers 82
Plantation Punch 60
Pom Pom 182
port
   Plantation Punch 60
   Whiskey Sangaree 74
Pretty In Pink 113
Prohibition Punch 160
Pussycat 31

Queen of Memphis 133

Ranch Girl 162
Raspberry Lemonade 118
Raspberry Mist 99
Rattlesnake 134
Red Apple Sunset 161

red wine: Sangria 146
rosé wine: Summer
   Punch 121
Royal Julep 102
Royal Silver 114
rum
   Apple Breeze 118
   Bajan Sun 60
   Banana Colada 56
   Banana Daiquiri 137
   Blue Hawaiian 61
   Caribbean
      Champagne 102
   Club Mojito 59
   Cuba Libre 64
   Cuban 80
   Cuban Special 64
   Daiquiri 56
   Disco Dancer 90
   Frozen Peach Daiquiri 66
   Hurricane 57
   Josiah's Bay Float 136
   Long Island Iced Tea 45
   Mai Tai 62
   Mellow Mule 137
   Ocean Breeze 61
   Palm Beach 22
   Piña Colada 58
   Plantation Punch 60
   Rum Cobbler 65
   Rum Cooler 67
   Rum Noggin 65
   Sparkling Gold 98
   Spotted Bikini 42
   Strawberry Colada 57
   Zombie 63

Sabrina 107
St. Clements 178
Saketini 34
Salty Dog 39
Salty Puppy 185
sambuca
   Black Beauty 42
   Tornado 141
   Zander 132
San Joaquin Punch 114
San Remo 98
Sangria 146
Sangria Seca 165
schnapps
   After Five 135
   Bloody Brain 129
   Fuzzy Navel 38
   High Voltage 125
   Minted Diamonds 136
   Peach Floyd 145
   Sex On The Beach 38
   The Bentley 99
   Tornado 141
   Voodoo 153
   White Diamond
      Frappé 141
   Woo-Woo 37
Screwdriver 51
Sloe Screw 131
Sea Breeze 50
Seelbach 110
Seventh Heaven 29
Sex On The Beach 38
Shady Lady 144
Shamrock 72
Shirley Temple 158
Sidecar 81
Silk Stockings 125
Singapore Sling 18
Slush Puppy 171
Sober Sunday 174
Soft Sangria 180
Southern Champagne 106
Southern Comfort
   A Sloe Kiss 21
   Alabama Slammer 152

Plantation Punch 60
   Southern Champagne 106
Sparkling Gold 98
Spotted Bikini 42
Strawberry Colada 57, 178
Summer Punch 121
Sunny Bay 49
Sunrise 181

Teardrop 30
tequila
   Bleu Bleu Bleu 31
   El Diablo 124
   El Toro 124
   Firefly 22
   High Voltage 125
   Long Island Iced Tea 45
   Shady Lady 144
   Silk Stockings 125
   Tequila Slammer 126
   Tequila Sunrise 127
Thai Fruit Cocktail 171
The Bentley 99
The Blue Train 33
The Gunner 176
The Queen's Cousin 111
The Reviver 78
The Stone Fence 116
Thistle 77
Thunderbird 47
Toffee Split 153
Tom Collins 19
Tornado 141
Tricolor 143
Triple Sec
   Banana Daiquiri 137
   Colleen 77
   Cosmopolitan 36
   Cuban Special 64
   Duke 94
   Hawaiian Orange
      Blossom 26
   Kamikaze 39
   Maiden's Prayer 23
   Royal Silver 114
   San Remo 98
   Seelbach 110
   Sidecar 81
   The Blue Train 33
   The Queen's Cousin 111
   Zombie 63

Under The Boardwalk 103

vermouth
   Amarettine 107
   Beadlestone 76
   Bloodhound 25
   Broken Negroni 110
   BVD 130
   Flying Scotsman 76
   Highland Fling 69
   Manhattan 73
   Martini 18
   Miami Beach 70
   Pink Whiskers 82
   Shamrock 72
   Thistle 77
   Virgin Mary 164
vodka
   A Sloe Kiss 21
   Black Beauty 42
   Black Russian 128
   Bleu Bleu Bleu 31
   Bloody Caesar 44
   Bloody Mary 44
   Blue Lagoon 140
   Blue Monday 43
   Chocolate Martini 152
   Cordless Screwdriver 43
   Cosmopolitan 36
   Cranberry Collins 50
   Flirtini 105

Flying Grasshopper 46
Fuzzy Navel 38
Harvey Wallbanger 40
Kamikaze 39
Kir Lethale 109
Last Mango in Paris 47
Long Island Iced Tea 45
Metropolitan 52
Midnight's Kiss 112
Mimi 48
Moscow Mule 51
Mudslide 149
Peach Floyd 145
Peartini 41
Salty Dog 39
Screwdriver 51
Sea Breeze 50
Sex On The Beach 38
Spotted Bikini 42
Sunny Bay 49
The Queen's Cousin 111
Thunderbird 47
Vodka Espresso 53
Woo-Woo 37
Voodoo 153

Wedding Belle 27
whiskey/whisky
   Beadlestone 76
   Boston Sour 71
   Bourbon Milk Punch 139
   Champagne Sidecar 91
   Colleen 77
   Flying Scotsman 76
   French Kiss 133
   Highland Fling 69
   Irish Coffee 155
   Klondike Cooler 72
   Manhattan 73
   Miami Beach 70
   Old-Fashioned 73
   Pink Heather 75
   Queen of Memphis 133
   Royal Julep 102
   Seelbach 110
   Shamrock 72
   The Stone Fence 116
   Thistle 77
   Whiskey Rickey 68
   Whiskey Sangaree 74
   Whiskey Sling 69
   Whiskey Sour 68
White Cosmopolitan 151
White Diamond Frappé 141
white wine
   Kamikaze 39
   Moonlight 28
white wine, sparkling
   Amarettine 107
   Black Velvet 101
   Broken Negroni 110
   Death In The... 111
   Disco Dancer 90
   Duke 94
   Kir Lethale 109
   Marilyn Monroe 115
   Midnight's Kiss 112
   Monte Carlo 104
   Night & Day 115
   Pink Heather 75
   Pink Sherbet Royale 108
   Pretty In Pink 113
   Raspberry Mist 99
   Royal Silver 114
   San Joaquin Punch 114
   Seelbach 110
   Tequila Slammer 126
   The Queen's Cousin 111
Wild Silk 100
Woo-Woo 37

Zander 132
Zombie 63